PROFILES OF A RABBI
Synoptic Opportunities in Reading About Jesus

Number 177
PROFILES OF A RABBI
Synoptic Opportunities in Reading About Jesus

by
Bruce Chilton

PROFILES OF A RABBI

Synoptic Opportunities in Reading About Jesus

by

The Revd Prof. Bruce Chilton

Bernard Iddings Bell Professor and Chaplain,
Bard College;
Rector, the Church of St John the Evangelist

Scholars Press
Atlanta, Georgia

PROFILES OF A RABBI
Synoptic Opportunities in Reading About Jesus

© 1989
Brown University

Library of Congress Cataloging in Publication Data

Chilton, Bruce.
   Profiles of a rabbi : synoptic opportunities in reading about
Jesus / by Bruce Chilton.
     p. cm. -- (Brown Judaic studies ; no. 177)
   Bibliography: p.
   Includes indexes.
   ISBN 1-55540-362-X (alk. paper)
   1. Synoptic problem. 2. Rabbinical literature--History and
criticism. 3. Rabbinical literature--Relation to the New Testament.
4. Bible. N.T. Gospels--Criticism, interpretation, etc.
I. Title. II. Series.
BS2555.2.C493 1989
226'.066--dc20   89-10307
                                          CIP

Printed in the United States of America
on acid-free paper

For the Revd Prof. John W. Rogerson

Contents

Preface

What lies before the reader is an attempt, along one line of development, to trace my growing dissatisfaction with the generally current approach to "the Synoptic Problem," and my nascent opinion that another approach is possible. In Part One, the rudiments of the Gospels' synopticity are reviewed, and the hypotheses of Markan priority and Matthean priority, their strengths and weaknesses, are described. That consideration brings me to the five Studies in Part Two, all of which compare passages in the Synoptic Gospels with instances of synopticity in Rabbinica. My conclusion is not that the Gospels and Rabbinica are directly comparable in literary terms, but that the phenomena which -- in aggregate -- make the Gospels unique are severally manifest in Rabbinica.

The Synoptic Gospels are catechetical instruments which are organically related in the material they present and in the order of their presentation. But they are not demonstrably explicable as the results of one Gospel's influence upon others, whether directly or indirectly. The supposition that they are genetically related is an artifact of discussion during the nineteenth century, not an inference from reading the Gospels and Rabbinica. Conclusions such as mine are commonly referred to the category of hypotheses of oral transmission, but even that supposition is here doubted. All that may be safely inferred from the synopticity of the Gospels is that they are mutually explicating: their catechetical function is the force which relates them, not anything that can be posited of "sources," "oral tradition," or "the historical Jesus." In that my cognitive approach involves setting aside geneticist language, a comparative language of analysis is here evolved, in order to permit discussion to continue.

The title expresses the thesis: I have grown to see that synopticity is only a "problem" within a mind set which would impose a genetic relationship upon documents which are not genetically related. Rightly approached, synopticity provides us with an occasion to read our texts more critically, and within the limits of our certainty. It took me a longer time than may have been thought necessary to develop my approach, because I was taught the "answer" to the "problem" before I knew what synopticity was. Such is often the fate of scholars of the New Testament.

Fortunately, when the scholarly guild may seem entrenched, students can provide fresh perspectives and insights. That has been my experience at Sheffield University, the Yale Divinity School, and Bard College. I thank all three institutions for their students, and the latter two for their excellent support in the area of computing. Jacob Neusner has graciously accepted my manuscript for publication, and I am grateful that scholars will have the opportunity to test the sort of analysis I have been trying over the years.

Finally, I should like to express my appreciation of what John Rogerson has done for me, and for the Department of Biblical Studies at Sheffield University. Left to their own devices, institutions of higher learning can -- and often do -- reduce their faculty to Tannaim, better at repeating knowledge than at framing it. Prof. Rogerson has not tolerated such a model of teaching, and his coming to Sheffield enabled me to get out from under the disproportionate burden of administration and teaching which had been imposed upon me. In return, I dedicate this book to him, and promise to remember his fine example in dealing with younger colleagues.

B. D. C.
Annandale-on-Hudson
New York

Part One: Introduction

A) THE MODERN DILEMMA OF "THE SYNOPTIC PROBLEM"

Study of the relationship among Matthew, Mark, and Luke has, almost universally during this century, taken place within the terms of reference of "the Synoptic Problem." Indeed, many scholars of the Gospels would take our first sentence as tautologous. It is axiomatic for them that the emergence of the Synoptics was the consequence of a genetic influence of document upon document, so that the relationship among the first three Gospels is best described by identifying the most original sources and charting their evolution into the texts we can read today. "The Synoptic Problem" is not only, then, the phrase we use to signal the literary relationship of certain texts. It is also the banner of a perspective, which sees that relationship as a problem, a complicated interaction of sources which can ultimately be named and described according to their place in the process of documentary cause and effect which produced the Gospels.

Logically, there is much to admire in the model of documentary generation which students of "the Synoptic Problem" presuppose in their analysis. A hypothesis of literary borrowing, which involves one author adapting another's manuscript, is easily entertained by those of us who have been educated on the basis of reading sources deemed to be classic, and then writing about them. (Indeed, it might not be coincidental that some of the most prominent contributors to "the Synoptic Problem" were initially trained as classicists. They brought with them not only an expertise in Greek and Latin, but the assumption that great texts naturally occasion commentary and interpretation. When we discuss the work of Prof. William Sanday's seminar at Oxford later, that influence of classicism will become obvious.) In principle, the hypothetical assumption is of the same order, whether one posits that Mark and "Q" were the original, independent entities, which were later edited by Matthew and Luke, or one posits that Matthew was the first Gospel, which was utilized by Luke prior to Mark's conflation of Matthew and

Luke. Both those theses, the first accepted by a (sometimes unreflective) majority of scholars, the latter by a vociferous and growing minority, represent elegant applications to the texts at hand of the axiom of the generation of documents from documents.

The two schools of thought which are founded upon that axiom, those of Markan priority and Matthean priority, vie with one another over their relative elegance. Markan priorists cannot imagine Mark as the last Gospel to be written: how could he have omitted the narratives of Jesus' birth and of his appearances as risen from the dead which are so richly provided by, and structurally central within, Matthew and Luke? Matthean priorists, on the other hand, regard with some scorn the necessary postulation of a "Q" by their antagonists: why, they ask, should we need to imagine a source of Jesus' sayings side by side with Mark, when those very sayings are to found in Matthew and Luke? (Of course, the battle concerning elegance is often waged over stylistic matters, but the global issues particularly mentioned here feature persistently in the literature.) The growing insistence in the debate between the two schools, however, has tended to obscure their common adherence to the axiom of the generation of document from document, and a corollary thereof.

The two schools differ merely in regard to the priority of Matthew or Mark, and in the regard to the existence of "Q:" that one document is the necessary and sufficient condition of another, is a postulate common to both points of view. That postulate's strength is attested by the predominance of its corollary in contemporary discussion. If one document leads directly to another, as both schools of priority would have it, then it is economical and reasonable to speak of the author of the second document personally depending upon the work of the author of the first document. In the case of the Gospels -- where what we know of authors is limited to the title (if that is what the titles indeed reflect) -- the result is that we speak of Mark abbreviating Matthew (on one hypothesis) or of Matthew expanding Mark (on another), and, *mutatis mutandis,* of other sources in similar terms. On either reading, what has transpired is the personification of texts into individual authors. Even in studies which do not consciously invoke the axiom of the generation of document from document, it is common to find scholars referring to Matthew, Mark, and Luke as persons (usually, "Evangelists"), without any apparent awareness that they are abstracting those authors according to the logic of the interplay between texts (the only cognitive reality available) and certain assumptions of "the Synoptic Problem". From the second paragraph of the present discussion, documentary personification has been indulged, within the description of schools of priority. It would be interesting to know how many readers are not consciously aware of a shift as one moves from the designation of documents to the personification of Evangelists.

Within this book, an author will never again be personified on the basis of a document (except when the positions of others are described). One document will never be assumed simply to be a function of another. The relationship among the first three Gospels will not be equated with "the Synoptic Problem," understood genetically as a soluble puzzle of direct, documentary influence. Our program is recommended by both positive and negative considerations.

Our negative considerations are all derived from constraints involved in the discipline of exegesis. If the aim of exegesis is to understand texts thoroughly, in their internal and external relations, then conclusions should be based upon the reader's cognition of those texts. Programs of study and investigation are commendable only insofar as the reader's cognition is advanced, although such programs -- complete with their operative hypotheses -- are perfectly admissible, provided they are illuminating. (It is, then, no surprise that exegetes are regularly both eclectic and relatively unsystematic in their craft.) But I cannot think of what I know better by equating the process of formation which lies behind a Gospel with people (about whom I have practically no information) called "Matthew," "Mark," or "Luke." As a matter of probability, such usage will make me less aware, not more so, of those problematic signs of variety and even contradiction which are characteristically apparent within each Gospel, and which may betray an emphatically communal authorship. If such language is defended as a mere convenience, my advice is that it is one of those conveniences which is, in the end, simply too expensive. Similarly, once I leave the world of individual authors neatly interpreting their manuscripts on desks they did not have, the axiom of the generation of document from document also looks dubious. Forces other than literary might shape a text, and those forces might be exerted within media other than writing, for example in oral tradition and the non-verbal approval or disapproval of a large audience. Finally, any number of literary, non-literary, and/or social forces might lay behind the formation of a given Gospel: to suppose that all the important "sources" lie to hand in (or within) the canonical Gospels is unwarranted. And so "the Synoptic Problem," the axiom of the generation of document from document, and the personification of documents all strike me as unnecessary and potentially misleading within exegetical terms of reference.

But there is also a more positive consideration, in view of which we might leave the perspective which places "the Synoptic Problem" at the center of attention in approaching the first three Gospels. Suppose -- if only for the sake of argument -- that we do not have all the pieces before us, which might be completed so as to form a puzzle without lacunae. There might well have been sources, written and/or oral, of which we have no inkling, and social forces, such as the expectations of audiences, which by their nature have left no trace today, although they were profoundly influential at the time the Gospels emerged. Under those circumstances, our "authors" and their mutual relations, whether plotted on the supposition of Matthean or of Mark priority, might be no more than artifacts of an inappropriate approach to the Gospels. Suppose -- in other words -- that the logic of searching for a solution to "the Synoptic Problem" has caused us to overlook an approach which is more cognate with the texts themselves. What might such an approach be? In order even to begin to address that question, we must review some of the data which have brought about a period of intense debate in the study of the Synoptic Gospels.

Were we to limit our imaginations to paradigms which have been proposed and investigated before, in some two hundred years of discussing "the Synoptic Problem," we would likely conclude, albeit with considerable qualification, that some form or another of the hypothesis of Markan priority is to be recommended. Such, in any case, has been the experience of most students of the Synoptic Gospels during the course of this century. But our suspicion that Markan priority is superior as a hypothesis among those which have been considered is not based upon others' experience alone. Our judgment is also based upon the regularity with which Mark appears as the common term within the Synoptics generally. Once Mark is found to be so, its relative lacunae (most notably, as mentioned, narratives of Jesus' birth and his appearance as risen) and its stylistic roughness give it a primitive air. Within a paradigm of the genetic dependence of one document upon another, Markan priority must appear a relatively straightforward inference, whatever problems are involved.

A brief review of the sorts of consideration which typically feature in a genetic approach is in order, so as to justify the remarks offered in the previous paragraph, and to serve as a foundation of our development of an alternative line of investigation. Perhaps the most striking feature of the Synoptic relationship is the frequency with which verbal identity, or near identity, is found in the Gospels. We might take as an example the following saying of Jesus, found only in the Synoptics:

Matthew 16:28
Amen I say to you that there are some of those standing here, such who will never taste death until they see the son of man coming in his kingdom

Mark 9:1
Amen I say to you that there are here some of
those standing, such who will never taste death
until they see the kingdom of God having come in
power

Luke 9:27
I say to you truly, there are some of those
standing there who will never taste death until
they see the kingdom of God.

The basic similarity of the sayings is evident, and is
specifically manifest in the following words, given in
the same order in each of the Gospels:

    a) I say to you
    b) there are some of those standing
    c) will never taste death
    d) until they see (the) kingdom.

At the same time, each of the Gospels deviates from
this common presentation of the saying:

    Matthew
    a) "Amen," "that"
    b) "here"
    c) "such who"
    d) "the son of man coming in his"

    Mark
    a) "Amen," "that"
    b) "here"
    c) "such who"
    d) "having come in power"

    Luke
    a) "truly"
    b) "there"
    c) "who"
    d) "of God."

Most   of   these   deviations   are   not   actually
peculiarities, however. The variant "Amen" is shared

by Matthew and Mark, and Luke's "truly" in a different position simply gives the equivalent meaning of the term (cf. Chilton, "Amen" [1978]). "That" and "here" are also held in common in Matthew and Mark (the latter in different positions); they also share "such who" in the "c" clause and a form of the verb "to come" in the "d" clause. Indeed, the only Matthean peculiarity is the reference to "the son of man," rather than the kingdom of God, as coming. Again, all Markan deviations from the common wording are held in common with Matthew, except for those in clause "d," where "of God" and "in power" appear. The first variant is held in common with Luke, while the latter is a genuine peculiarity. Luke's "truly" in "a" and his "who" in "c" are variants which do not alter the meaning of the saying and "of God" in "d" is held in common with Mark. "There," however, in "b" is a genuine peculiarity.

Each of these Gospels, then, presents a slight peculiarity in its presentation of the saying. ("Slight" is used here to describe the numerically small departure from the common wording, not to claim that the peculiarity is insignificant. The question of the significance of deviations which are only noted at the moment will be explored by means of Studies in Part Two.) Most of the words actually used, however, are held in common among the first three Gospels, and most deviations from the common wording are shared by two of the Gospels. In the following diagram of the position, common wording is presented in roman type, while deviations and peculiarities are placed in italics:

    a) Mt: *Amen* I say to you *that*
          Mk: *Amen* I say to you *that*
          Lk: I say to you *truly*

    b) Mt: there are some of those standing *here*
          Mk: there are *here* some of those standing
          Lk: there are some of those standing *there*

 c)   Mt: *such who* will never taste death
      Mk: *such who* will never taste death
      Lk: *who* will never taste death

 d)   Mt: until they see the *son of man coming in his* kingdom
      Mk: until they see the kingdom *of God having come in power*
      Lk: until they see the kingdom *of God.*

In this case, then, the near identity of wording among the three Gospels is the most striking feature, and even deviations are regularly shared. The pattern of these shared deviations should be noted: although most of the deviations (in "a," "b," and "c") are presented commonly by Matthew and Mark, leaving Luke to the side, the most startling deviation (in "d," the reference to the son of man or the kingdom) aligns Mark and Luke against Matthew. Mark appears to provide a verbally median version of the saying, having elements in common with Matthew and Luke which Matthew and Luke do not themselves share.

This pattern of deviations, with Mark seeming to serve as the median term between Matthew and Luke, is largely maintained when we consider the texts of the Synoptic Gospels as a whole. In triply attested material, most of Mark's wording appears in Matthew and Luke, as in the example above. Indeed, it has been estimated that 51% of Mark's words within such passages appears in Matthew and that 53% of its words appear in Luke (Caird [1972] 18). For several reasons, however, we should be circumspect in evaluating such statistics. At first sight, such precise verbal agreement might seem to constitute conclusive proof that one "Evangelist" has actually copied the work of another in a slavish way. To draw such an inference without further reflection would, however, be rash. In the first place, it must be remembered that these statistics, frequently cited, refer only to the Synoptic material which is triply attested. They take no account of the substantial material which is peculiar to each of the Gospels, or of the extensive matter Mark does not present which Matthew and Luke have in common (see below). Were these factors taken into account, the verbatim agreement would fall to less than 25%. Secondly, the statistics are arrived at by an arithmetical computation of all the words involved, including "he said," "and," "but," "Jesus," etc. The common usage of such terms by the "Evangelists" is scarcely a matter of note. Thirdly, the statistics do not account for variations in the order and syntax of common wording, a factor which must be held to reduce their substantively verbatim identity. Lastly, the statistics include words which are similar, not only those which are identical. In short, the statistics reflect substantial verbal similarity, but not actually verbatim agreement.

None of these cautionary reflections, however. can explain away the statistics carefully compiled by John C. Hawkins (1909 and 1968) and frequently cited since his time. They underline the extent of the verbal agreement which any account of the Synoptic relationship must adequately explain. Moreover, they make it apparent that Mark occupies a central position in this verbal agreement. The second Gospel is something of a median term between Matthew and Luke; in the example cited, we have seen that Matthew and Mark agree to some extent against Luke, and that Luke and Mark to a lesser extent agree against Matthew, but Matthew and Luke never agree against Mark.

Our example is, to a limited extent, typical of the verbal relationship among the Gospels, but there are two important respects in which it is not typical. There is in the first place an important range of material (described below) which Matthew and Luke present, but not Mark. Obviously, the verbal relationship just described does not obtain in the case of such material. The second observation under cuts the generalization that Mark is the median term in the Synoptic relationship even more directly: there are cases in triply attested material where Matthew and Luke agree against Mark. Such cases are called minor agreements. In the example which follows (Matthew 13:11; Mark 4:11; Luke 8:10), minor agreements are given in italics:

Mt: *But* answering he *said*, To you it has been given *to know* the myster*ies* of the kingdom of the heavens, but to those it has not been given

Mk: And he was saying to them, To you the mystery has been given of the kingdom of God, but to those outside, everything comes in parables

Lk: *But* he *said*, To you it has been given *to know* the myster*ies* of the kingdom of God, but to the rest it is in parables.

Agreements of this kind are called "minor" because they occur less often than the triple agreements we have already mentioned, and because they are not usually the dominant feature of a given passage. (Cf. Hawkins [1909] 208-212, where they are estimated as constituting 21 cases.) In the present instance, there is peculiarity in each version of the saying (e.g., the last clause of each), and also agreement of Matthew and Mark against Luke (e.g., the use of the term "those") and of Mark and Luke against Matthew (e.g., the use of the term "parables"). This illustrates the fact that the verbal relationship among the Synoptic Gospels is complex; no one Gospel escapes from agreeing and disagreeing with the other two. While Mark appears to be the median term in the relationship, in the sense that its wording is on average the most common wording of triply attested material, it does not always present the common wording. For this reason, it is misleading to call Mark the "middle term" between Matthew and Luke, such that Mark links the wording of Matthew and Luke in triply attested material (cf. Styler [1966] 225). In logic, the phrase "middle term" is used to denote that which is implied within the premises of a syllogism; obviously, it will not do to assume Markan priority, however much it may appear a straightforward inference within the paradigm of "the Synoptic Problem." The second Gospel is only the median or average term which gives us a point of entry into the verbal agreement among the Gospels when that agreement is most striking. Mark's wording is therefore of particular interest, but by itself it cannot explain the Synoptic relationship. Such dictional relations (along with relations of content and of order) are simply one of the three principal categories of phenomena which need to be accounted for.

The position is similar when we consider the matter (or content) which the Synoptic Gospels have in common. John C. Hawkins, whose statistics have frequently been cited in the course of discussion, estimated that Luke contains 499 "peculiar" verses out of a total of 1,149, in other words, roughly 43% is original as compared to Matthew and Mark (Hawkins [1909] 25). Of Matthew's 1,068 verses, in Hawkins's reckoning 338, or 32%, are original (p. 10), while he considers that only 50 of Mark's 661 verses, or just under 8%, are original (p. 14). From these observations, it follows immediately that Mark is the most representative of the Synoptic Gospels in the material which it presents. As in the case of wording, however, we need to resist the temptation to read too much into that general statement. Some 92% of Mark is paralleled in Matthew and Luke together; when the latter two Gospels are looked at individually, the picture appears somewhat different. A slightly greater number of Mark's verses (55, or just over 8%) are not found paralleled in Matthew, although 24 of these are to be found in Luke (Streeter [1924] 169). The situation is globally different, however, when Luke is considered in comparison to Mark, to some extent because seventy-four consecutive verses in Mark (6:45-8:26, omitting 7:16 as a textual variant) find no parallel in Luke (Streeter [1924] 172). But altogether some 311 verses in Mark, or 47%, find no analogy in Luke (Streeter [1924] 160), so that the Lukan rate of correspondence to Mark is dramatically less than the Matthean rate. Indeed, these rates of correspondence are so different that we are only just correct in claiming that Mark is a mean term between Matthew and Luke in respect of the matter presented. In respect of wording, Mark is also "median" in the sense that the second Gospel is largely (but not always) found in a mediating position in the verbal correspondence among the first three Gospels. This is not so consistently the case where the materials contained in the Gospels are concerned. Of course, the place of Mark as the most common Gospel cannot be disputed: the statistics only confirm it. But Luke's rate of material correspondence to Mark so nearly approaches 50% that Mark barely manages to be "average" or "mean" in respect of Luke, and this robs Mark of a truly median position between Matthew and Luke.

Mark therefore represents the principal, mean term in the Synoptic material as well as the largely median term in the Synoptic wording. There is, however, another important mean term in respect of the material presented by Matthew, Mark and Luke. Such material is commonly called "Q," from the German word "Quelle," which means source. (There are alternative explanations of how the siglum, "Q," arose by the end of the last century, but they do not account as well for its wide recognition.) The word "source" normally implies that a written document is at issue, but even B.H. Streeter -- the leading exponent of a documentary theory of the Synoptic relationship -- admitted that oral tradition provided at least some of the material which Matthew and Luke have in common against Mark (Streeter [1924] 184). This doubly attested material should not be confused with the minor agreements, which are sporadic, verbal similarities between Matthew and Luke against Mark in triply attested material. By material in "Q" we mean such passages as the preaching of John the Baptist, the extensive account of Jesus' temptation (including his dialogue with the devil), the long discourse commonly called the sermon on the mount, the story of the healing of the centurion's servant, John's question whether Jesus is the one that is to come, and many well known sayings of Jesus (cf. Streeter [1924] 273-294). The paucity of narrative material in this alleged source, oral or written, is perhaps troublesome when one tries to imagine what it was used for before it was included in Matthew and Luke. Streeter (pp. 291-292) attempted to explain it by analogy to a Prophetic book of the

Hebrew Bible such as Jeremiah. He compared the baptism and temptation to prophetic "call" narratives, and pointed out that the Prophetic books consist largely of teaching. More recently, scholars such as Paul Hoffman (1972) and Siegfried Schulz (1972) have attempted to explain "Q" as a document of the early Church in or near Palestine, where concern grew to put Jesus' sayings in the context of the awakening apocalyptic trend which was influencing both Christianity and Judaism. This would explain the emphasis in "Q" on how and when Jesus would come as the judge at the end time.

While German discussion -- and, to a somewhat lesser extent, American discussion (cf. Edwards [1976], which presupposes a corpus of material) -- has largely proceeded on the assumption of "Q"'s existence, English discussion has been more skeptical. Austin Farrer's article, "On Dispensing with Q," gave voice to growing suspicions about "Q," and since its publication in 1955 several alternative theories, a few of which are to be discussed below, have been offered. To a great extent, some doubt is justified. Although one can speculate as to the origin and purpose of "Q" on the assumption it existed, there is absolutely no direct evidence that it actually did exist. During the nineteenth century, the attempt was made to identify "Q" with the *logia* of Jesus which Papias in the second century ascribed to Matthew. Indeed, that identification resulted in the term *logia* (singular: *logion*) being applied to Jesus' sayings. *Logion*, however, is a Greek word with a wide range of meanings, of which one is "revelation," not "saying," so that what Papias says Matthew wrote cannot be identified with "Q" on the basis of its title. More importantly, Papias appears in context (cf. Eusebius, *The History of the Church* 3.39) to be speaking of the canonical Gospel according to Matthew, as he goes on to speak of the Gospels of other "Evangelists." Without the attestation of Papias, there is no external testimony to the existence of a document which is alleged to have served as a fundamental source of the teaching of Jesus for Matthew and for Luke. That a document of such importance would not be

explicitly mentioned in the evidence of early
Christianity which remains is, of course, possible.
Luke, after all, does mention the work of anonymous
predecessors in its preface (1:2). The lack of a
single open reference to "Q" is therefore not fatal to
the hypothesis, although is does nothing to help it.
As we have already observed, even Streeter was not
prepared to claim that all of the material Matthew and
Luke have in common against Mark derived from a
single, written document. He allowed of the influence
of oral tradition in the cases in which the verbal
agreement between parallel passages is small, and
acknowledged that the hypothesis of "Q" requires a
degree of assumption (Streeter [1924] 184).

     Even on that assumption, Streeter admits that
the boundaries of "Q" are impossible exactly to
determine, that distinct versions of "Q" may have been
available to Matthew and Luke, and that Matthew and
Luke use "Q" in differing orders and contexts (pp.
184-185, 273-292). The hypothesis of "Q" as an actual
document looks even weaker when it is pointed out by
Streeter that some fifty verses in Mark "overlap" the
material of "Q". If the material of Mark and "Q" is
regarded as contiguous, the justification for
supposing that there are multiple, documentary sources
is far from evident. Such overlapping material is
generally longer and rougher in "Q" according to
Streeter; but the degree of difference between the
Markan and "Q" versions caused him to doubt Mark knew
"Q" in written form at all (p. 187). (Streeter's
ambivalence in regard to Mark's knowledge of "Q" will
concern us further as we proceed.) Moreover, on
Streeter's view that "Q" comprised 200 verses, Mark
would for some reason have used only 25% of the
material, and would have devoted less than 8% of his
Gospel to it. Matthew, on the other hand, gives just
under 19% of his space to a 200 verse "Q" and Luke
just over 17% of his space. Hawkins ([1909] 110)
assigns 191 "Q" verses to Matthew, or 18% of the
Gospel, and 181 "Q" verses to Luke, or some 16% of the
Gospel. The basic point still stands: Mark has much
less contact with "Q" on the assumption it existed.
The degree of correspondence between Matthew and Luke

is at the end of the day too significant to be overlooked. Indisputably, they have important material in common which Mark does not present: the existence of the material of "Q," whatever one might say of the hypothetical document called "Q," is an established fact. But the variations of wording and order between Matthew's "Q" Luke's "Q" (cf. Bowman [1961-1962]), as well as the question of Mark's relationship to either, make it problematic to assume "Q" was an actual document. Indeed, the material of "Q" is more a microcosm of the Synoptic relationship than an explanation of it.

Along with the wording they present and the matter they contain, the first three Gospels are synoptic in respect of the order which they follow. The category "order" is a literary one. One can, of course, make the general observation that the Synoptic Gospels present the ministry of Jesus according to the same basic pattern, at least from the moment of his baptism. He is pictured as preaching, making disciples, healing and encountering more and more opposition during a generally successful period in Galilee. This period is climaxed by Jesus' question to his disciples, "Who do people, and you in particular, think I am?' (cf. Matthew 16:13-15; Mark 8:27-29a; Luke 9:18-20a). Peter's response, to the effect that Jesus is messiah (Matthew 16:16; Mark 8:29b; Luke 9:20b) is followed by the first in a sequence of statements of Jesus in which he speaks of his own suffering, death and resurrection (Matthew 16:21; Mark 8:31; Luke 9:22). Significantly, the transfiguration, which follows, refers to a divine voice which confirms Jesus' identity (Matthew 17:5; Mark 9:7; Luke 9:35). From a literary point of view, the voice at the transfiguration is symmetrical with the baptismal voice (cf. Matthew 3:17; Mark 1:11; Luke 3:22). In effect, the transfiguration marks the next major period in Jesus' ministry (cf. Part II, Study 2). Jerusalem now appears increasingly as the goal of the peripatetic ministry as Jesus' teaching is expressed increasingly in the context of controversy. The opposition to Jesus finally culminates in the decision of the religious authorities to put him to death. From this moment (Matthew 26:1-5; Mark 14:1-2; Luke 22:1-2), the first three Gospels present accounts of Jesus' death, collectively known as the passion narrative, which contain less divergent material than is usual in a sequence which varies less than is usual. Until the notice of the empty tomb, there is excellent agreement among the Synoptic Gospels in respect of wording, matter and order, although there are important deviations, especially evident in Luke, in all three of these respects. Mark's ending states openly that Jesus has risen from the dead (16:6); in different ways, and now using unusually distinctive material, Matthew and Luke go on to speak of actual appearances of the risen Jesus. (The strong similarity of the three passion narratives, which is striking even within the Synoptic relation, has led many scholars to speak of a single narrative which Matthew, Mark and Luke all used.) The presentation of Jesus' ministry, with two distinct periods, each beginning with the authorization of a divine voice, and culminating respectively in Peter's confession and the disciples' response to the dead and risen Jesus, is common to the Synoptic Gospels. It distinguishes them qualitatively from the Johannine portrait.

The category of "order," however, refers to more than the general remarks which can be made about the pattern of Jesus' ministry in the Synoptic Gospels as compared to the fourth Gospel. Under this category we also refer to the actual sequence of passages, one after another, in Matthew, Mark and Luke, and to the fact that this literary sequence is so similar and yet -- once again -- distinctive. By way of example, we might consider the sequence of passages which deal with the beginning of Jesus' public ministry. The material which leads up to this first preaching is triply attested, with some additions from "Q," and matter unique to Luke:

a) The appearance of John the Baptist (Matthew 3:1-6; Mark 1:2-6; Luke 3:1-6)

b) His preaching of repentance (Matthew 3:7-10; Luke 3:7-9)

c) His ethical teaching (Luke 3:10-14)

d) His preaching of one who is stronger (Matthew 3:11-12; Mark 1:7-8; Luke 3:15-18)

e) His imprisonment (Luke 3:19-20; cf. Matthew 14:3-12; Mark 6:17-29)

f) The baptism of Jesus (Matthew 3:13-17; Mark 1:9-11; Luke 3:21-22)

g) Jesus' genealogy (Luke 3:23-38; cf. Matthew 1:1-17)

h) The temptation of Jesus (Matthew 4:1-11; Mark 1:12-13; Luke 4:1-13).

The extent to which the sequences of Matthew, Mark and Luke concur here is striking. The concurrence is manifest in triply attested material (cf. a, d, f, h) and in "Q" (cf. b and the dialogue in h, Matthew 4:3-11; Luke 4:3-13). The peculiarly Lukan material (c, e and g) finds a more or less reasonable place within the common sequence. (The placement of the genealogy in Luke is quite unlike that of the very different list given by Matthew in its first chapter, and is intended to balance Jesus' acclamation as God's son in 3:22 with a notice of who people thought Jesus was.) Luke's mention of John's imprisonment (e) here, however, is rather odd, for reasons we must now discuss. The oddity of the placement makes the notice appear peculiar within Luke, although the content of the statement is triply attested.

    Luke's notice of John's arrest by Herod is much shorter than Matthew's and Mark's; indeed, it provides no actual account of John's death. The placement of Luke's notice is also strange. Coming as it does immediately before the story of Jesus' baptism, one might conclude Jesus was baptized by someone else. In fact, while Matthew (3:13-15) and Mark (1:9) specifically speak of John as the agent of Jesus' baptism, Luke has no such reference (3:21).

The reason for this at first sight mysterious
reticence is not difficult to discover. Luke's Gospel
is presented together with the book of Acts, where the
story of the Church after the ascension is taken up
(cf. 1:1-11). Within that story, Luke--Acts relates
the teaching of a Jew named Apollos, who came from
Alexandria (18:24). Although he is described as
instilling the way of the Lord, as speaking with
spiritual zeal, and even as speaking accurately of
Jesus, Apollos is said only to recognize the baptism
of John (18:25). He is represented as being corrected
by Priscilla, Aquila (18:26), and (indirectly) by Paul
(19:1-7). The precise nature of Apollos' omission in
his preaching is not specified, but Paul's response to
some of Apollos' disciples makes it quite clear that
what is in question is a defective view of baptism in
which the reception of the spirit is not understood to
take place (19:2-4). This defective understanding is
linked with an overly enthusiastic appeal to the
example of John the Baptist, and a failure to
recognize that John merely prepared the way for Jesus
(cf. vv. 3-4). Once corrected, the disciples accept
baptism in Jesus' name and then receive the spirit,
after the example of the Twelve (vv. 5-7). The exact
nature of Apollos' teaching about John is not
mentioned, and in any case, the characterization of it
in Acts might well be doubted. Nonetheless, it is
quite apparent that Acts takes some pains to stress
that John was a purely preparatory figure in relation
to Jesus. On this basis, the placement of the notice
of John's imprisonment in the Gospel is explicable,
although the presentation -- explicable or not --
appears clumsy in comparison with Matthew and Luke.

So far, the picture that has emerged in the
example considered above is one in which the Synoptic
Gospels follow a largely common order, but that there
are important exceptions. The most notable of these
are from Luke's Gospel, where unique material occupies
an important and unusual position (cf. especially
3:23-38), and where even triply attested material
occupies a peculiar and at first sight inexplicable
position. In addition, the material in "Q," although
commonly placed in Matthew and Luke, breaks the

pattern of sequential agreement among all three Synoptic Gospels.

The accounts presented of the actual beginning of Jesus' public preaching ministry differ remarkably. Matthew 4:12-17 speaks of Jesus' coming to Galilee after John's arrest in order to preach the kingdom. This activity is held by Matthew to "fulfill" a statement made by the prophet Isaiah (vv. 14-16). The context of Jesus' preaching in Mark is specified much as it is in Matthew: after John's arrest and in Galilee (1:14). But there is no citation of scripture, and the words cited as the content of Jesus' preaching do not accord fully with those given in Matthew (cf. Mark 1:15 and Matthew 4:17). Luke has no reference to John in this context, as we might have expected, although it does place the action in Galilee, with Jesus' arrival there motivated by the spirit (4:14). A general reference to a ministry of teaching is followed by the first example of Jesus' preaching, beginning with a reading at a sabbath service in Nazareth and ending with the congregation's attempt to execute him (vv.15-30). This picture of rejection leading to further missionary activity (cf. vv. 31f.) accords with the pattern of the Church's ministry in Acts (cf. especially 8:1-3; 13:14-14:6 and Chilton [1979] 123-156). Jesus does not even mention the kingdom of God in his inaugural preaching, although Luke presupposes that the kingdom was the burden of his message (4:43).

From this point onward, variations of sequence which are more marked than those we have already noted become apparent:

a) Jesus' first preaching (Matthew 4:12-17; Mark 1:14-15; Luke 4:14-30)

b) His call of disciples (Matthew 4:18-22; Mark 1:16-20; cf. Luke 5:1-11)

c) The exorcism at Capernaum (Mark 1:21-28; Luke 4:31-37)

d) The healing of Peter's mother-in-law (Mark
1:29-31; Luke 4:38-39, cf. Matthew 8:14, 15)

e) The healing of many (Mark 1:32-34; Luke
4:40-41, cf. Matthew 8:16, 17)

f) Jesus' departure for a wider ministry (Matthew
4:23; Mark 1:35-39; Luke 4:42-44).

The relationship among the first three Gospels, even
within the short run of passages mentioned, is more
complicated than our scheme of presentation would
suggest. But before we speak of those complications,
the basic pattern that has emerged is worth
considering: where the three Synoptic Gospels do not
agree in the sequence of the material they have in
common, then either Matthew and Mark agree against
Luke (as in b), or Mark and Luke agree against Matthew
(c, d, e). It must be emphasized that this
generalization applies only to triply attested
material, but in such material Mark is indeed the
middle term which links the order of Matthew and that
of Luke, when they are related, and which consistently
presents the most common order along with Matthew
and/or Luke.
       As Streeter observed ([1924] 166), Matthew and
Mark generally agree in order, with the additional or
different Matthean material slotted in at the
appropriate place. In the present case Matthew 4:12-17
is much fuller than Mark 1:14-15 ("a"), and Matthew
4:23 is more economical than, and differs in its
emphasis from, Mark 1:35-39 ("f"). Despite these
variations, the basic sequence (preaching, call,
healing and departure) is maintained. The apparent
absence of Matthean parallels to "c," "d" and "e" is
purely a function of the fact that we have restricted
our attention to a short run of passages. Phrases in
"c," the exorcism at Capernaum, are paralled in
Matthew 4:24 (cf. Mark 1:28 and Luke 4:37) and
7:28b-29 (cf. Mark 1:22; Luke 4:32), although the
story as a whole does not appear in Matthew. Passages
"d" and "e" are more completely paralleled in chapter

eight of Matthew (vv. 14-17, as indicated above), and
in that sequence, so that a complete break in order
does not occur. Nonetheless, Matthew presents the
curiosity that it emphasizes Jesus' healing ministry
in a summary passage (4:23-24) before it cites a
specific example of his healing activity.

Streeter described the Lukan order in different
terms ([1924] 167). He observed the close agreement in
certain sections, as in the present case (4:14f.),
while in others (e.g. 3:1-4:13, our earlier example)
he claimed a different sequence was the primary
influence. To argue, however, for a qualitatively
different principal of order in Luke 3:1-4:13 as
compared to 4:14-44 is problematic. Although there are
important additions and striking distinctions in the
former passage, the same observation applies to the
latter. Luke's "a" passage, the description of Jesus'
inaugural preaching, is quite unlike its analogues in
Matthew and Mark. The omission of any reference to the
preaching of the kingdom, especially in view of 4:43,
is particularly noticeable, and implies a certain
tension with the understanding of Matthew and Mark
that the kingdom, rather than his own view of himself
as messiah, was the foundation of Jesus' initial
preaching. The next passage in Luke which parallels
Mark is the story of the exorcism at Capernaum (vv.
31-37). The very fact that there is such a substantive
parallel to Mark 1:21-28, while Matthew's coincidence
with Mark is quite incomplete, evidences Luke's
similarity to Mark, and the sequential agreement from
"c" through "f" only confirms their similarity. This
pattern of coincidence is shattered, however, by the
omission of "b" in Luke, which Matthew and Mark share.
In 5:1-11 Luke does present a call story which is
quite different in substance from "b," but -- had it
been presented after "a" -- we would have said that it
was comparable enough to the Matthean and Markan
presentations to say that Luke agreed with the order
of its colleagues even though the material presented
was distinctive. That Luke failed to do so means it
departs from the common order not only in the
placement of an important passage, but also in the
thematic structure established by Matthew and Mark in

the sequence of passages at the opening of Jesus'
ministry. Although the Matthean presentation has a
truncated version of the third element in the sequence
of preaching, call, healing and departure, it is not
completely displaced, so that the thematic patterning
agrees with that of Mark. Luke's complete omission of
a call passage from this sequence gives an altogether
different emphasis and tone to the section.

In describing one Synoptic Gospel in comparison
with another, particularly as regards order, one
naturally uses such terms as "displacing," "truncated
version," as well as "abbreviation," "elaboration,"
"tranposition," "omission," "addition," etc. The use
of language of this sort is almost an inevitable
consequence of comparing one document to others, and
synoptic comparison is the best means at our disposal
for characterizing the first three Gospels as
individual works, and as representations of a unique
genre. But the fact that we can use such language
should not lead us to assume, for example, that Mark
is a deliberate abbreviation of Matthew, or that
Matthew is an intentional elaboration of Mark. To do
so would permit a mere convention of speech and
analysis to dictate the way in which we see the actual
history of the texts' development. Only in Part III
will we turn to the question of how the Synoptic
Gospels came to have the relationship they do.

For the moment, however, it is plain enough that
Mark might be described as the "average" Gospel among
the Synoptics. Its wording is largely median, its
order more exactly so, and its content is mean as
compared to Matthew and Luke. Within a genetic
paradigm, Mark most readily occupies the beginning or
the end in a progression of development. Predictably,
that is precisely what the schools of Markan and
Matthean priority respectively do posit. The Achilles'
heel of Markan priority, enthusiastically exploited by
Matthean priorists, consists of the material which the
theory does not easily account for. If "Q" is a source
distinct from Mark, why is there an "overlap" of
anything like 25%? If Matthew and Luke independently
redacted Mark and "Q," why do they present "minor
agreements"? Of course, when Matthean priorists

attempt to build an alternative hypothesis out of the "minor agreements," they must then explain Mark's failure to use a great deal of material, and the appearance of stylistic roughness in the second Gospel. For that reason, Markan priority is widely and yet cautiously recommended by most scholars of the Gospels today.

The relative strength of the hypothesis of Markan priority, however, cannot conceal a fundamental weakness. It is only strong when the axiom of the generation of document from document and its corollary are invoked, and then it is only comparatively strong, when balanced against the hypothesis of Matthean priority. The overlap of "Q" with Mark and the "minor agreements" persistently challenge the comprehensiveness of the theory, while the regular appearance of Mark as the mean and/or median term within the Synoptic Gospels highlights it as in some way central within the relationship of them all. Meanwhile, the logical possibility of positing that Mark is the average Gospel because it is a conflation of Matthew and Luke seems less than plausible exegetically, since it involves the supposition that much rich material was deliberately omitted in the redaction of Mark.

The language of the day would have it that the "paradigm" of literary dependence results in "anomalies" when applied to our texts themselves, with the result that a "paradigm shift" may be necessary. Analysis of that kind was spelled out by Thomas S. Kuhn in his book, *The Structure of Scientific Revolutions* (1962), and has widely been applied within biblical studies. Indeed, it may be argued that our application of Kuhn's language has been somewhat indiscriminate, in that many new ideas (and several old ones) have been clothed in "paradigm shifts," whether or not a new perspective on the field generally is in fact involved. Kuhn's language should be reserved for alterations of the conceptual framework within which we operate, such that the new framework cannot be articulated from within the old. Obviously, most changes of paradigm will, at the time they occur, simply seem to most observers a period of

confusion. Whether such confusion is caused by the
creative tensions from which new paradigms of
cognition emerge, or by the periodic ineptitude of
researchers, is something which will only be
determined with time and subsequent evaluation. To
speak blithely of shifting paradigms, as if they could
be taken off and put on at will, is to miss the point.
Kuhn's reference is to the consciousness with which we
perceive our world, not to an assortment of bright
ideas. Likewise, Kant's language of antinomies is
probably not in order, since it is not clear that we
have exhausted our conventional logic in analyzing the
Gospels.

A fresh approach to the relationship among
Matthew, Mark, and Luke need not, therefore, invoke
anomalies or antinomies in any formal sense. But we
might more modestly claim that a fixation with
literary dependence, associated with the axiom of the
generation of document from document and the corollary
of documentary personification, has unduly limited the
perspective of contributors to "the Synoptic Problem,"
with the result that different sorts of relationship,
evidenced in nearly contemporaneous literature, have
not been investigated. (In the ordinary sense that an
alteration of model is here explored, a change of
paradigm may in fact be spoken of, albeit not with the
technical meaning Kuhn has popularized.) In order to
assess that possibility, the next section of the
Introduction will be devoted to a road not taken at
the turn of the century, during the period of classic
discussion of "the Synoptic Problem." We focus our
attention upon certain scholars of that time, not
because others are not important (indeed, some later
works must also be mentioned here), but because our
concern is more with the logic of analysis than with
the history of study.

B) A ROAD NOT TAKEN

In England, a solution of "the Synoptic Problem" which H. J. Holtzmann (1863) proposed excited great interest. Building upon the observations of Karl Lachmann earlier in the century (1835), Holtzmann concluded that, since Mark is the most common term among the Synoptics, any earlier source of the narrative of all three must have been most like Mark. That hypothetical entity was called "Ur-Marcus," and Holtzmann also postulated the existence of "Q." The virtue of the proposal was not the originality of its elements, but its simplicity. With signal modifications, it was destined to overtake Griesbach's theory of Matthean priority, still the most widely accepted at the time Holtzmann wrote. Those modifications, and the emergence of Markan priority as a practical assumption within study in the twentieth century, are more attributable to William Sanday than to any other single person. Between 1894 and 1910, Sanday, who held successive professorships at Oxford University, convened a seminar to investigate the issues involved in Holtzmann's hypothesis. The published result was *Oxford Studies in the Synoptic Problem* (1911). Sanday had been attracted to Holtzmann's solution because of its simplicity, its usefulness as an account of the evidence, but also for another reason. The so-called "Tübingen School" in Germany, at first under the guidance of F. C. Baur, had attempted to explain the New Testament in a way which questioned its historicity. The documents of primitive Christianity were not seen as based on reliable tradition, but as under the influence of dogmatic interests. They might seem to be historical, but in fact they were the projection of ideas. D. F. Strauss, in his celebrated life of Jesus, referred to such historicizing projections as "myths." But if Ur-Marcus, the principal source of the Synoptics, is seen as the account Papias said Mark wrote from Peter's dictation (cf. Eusebius, *The History of the Church* 2.15), then the primitive character of the Gospels is established. Such an understanding suited

Sanday's informed impression of the New Testament as a whole.

The Oxford seminar, however, went a fateful step further. While Holtzmann had argued that Ur-Marcus was the principal source of the first three Gospels, F. H. Woods and B. H. Streeter held that Mark itself was the source of Matthew and of Luke (cf. Farmer [1976] 63-67 and Streeter [1924]). The seminar, then, marked the birth of the classic, "two-source" solution of the Synoptic Problem. With their simplification, Woods and Streeter reduced the number of hypothetical documents further still (as compared to Holtzmann), so that it was much more like Griesbach's solution than other solutions which involve hypothetical documents. They also succeeded in removing one stage between the "Evangelists" and the most primitive Christian tradition; indeed Mark was itself a representative of that tradition on their understanding.

Their enthusiasm for their position led Woods and Streeter to argue its logical superiority to Griesbach's solution, although Streeter acknowledged that their alternative could not actually be proved. In fact, Streeter went on (1924) to posit a solution involving four sources. In his argument, the extra material in Matthew and Luke -- as compared to Mark -- could be explained on the assumption that there was an earlier recension of Luke, a "proto-Luke," and that Matthew had access to certain special traditions. To an extent, then, Streeter's solution engaged in the sort of multiplication of sources which Holtzmann's was designed to avoid, although the priority of canonical Mark to Matthew and Luke remains its distinctively new element. But one argument put forward by Woods and Streeter, in favor of Markan priority, was unfortunate. Karl Lachmann had observed that Mark presents the common order of the Synoptics, and he rightly inferred that -- if a source was used by the "Evangelists" -- its order approximated that of Mark most closely. But it is not logical to say, as Woods and Streeter did, that because Mark has the common order, it must be the source of Matthew and Luke. One can say equally that Mark's common order is the result of copying Matthew and Luke, as in

Griesbach's solution.

The quasi-logical argument came during the course of the century to be used to give Markan priority the aura of rational proof. Once the fallacy was spotted, however, the entire solution was brought into disrepute. Somewhat unfairly, it became known as the "Lachmann fallacy," even though Lachmann himself did not perpetrate it. Long after Streeter's solution had become a standard feature of teaching in higher education, B. C. Butler called attention to the failure in logic in his attempt to establish *The Originality of St. Matthew* (1951). The most lucid account of how the fallacy arose, and of how it influenced generations of students and scholars, was contributed by W. R. Farmer in *The Synoptic Problem* (1964, 1976). Since the publication of his book, discussion of the Synoptic Gospels has been in ferment.

Farmer's book is presented in two, very distinctive parts; both merit attention here, for the light they shed on the work and logic of Sanday's seminar. The first part is a discussion of the history of research into the Synoptic Problem, and it is noted for the fluency of its presentation. Although the discussion is very succinct, Farmer skilfully, and sometimes allusively, relates arguments made by scholars in respect of the Synoptic Problem to their positions on other issues of note within the study of the New Testament. The question of the historical reliability of the Gospels, for example, seems to have influenced Sanday in his appreciation for Holtzmann. On the other hand, Farmer's zeal for Griesbach's solution sometimes leads him to present the hypothesis of Markan priority in an unfair light. He claims that the position of Holtzmann gained favor simply because it enabled the historicity of Mark to be maintained. In fact, however, scholars turned to the leading alternative to Griesbach's hypothesis during the nineteenth century because a careful comparison of parallel texts turned up phenomena which were difficult to explain on Griesbach's account (cf. Tuckett [1983]). Moreover, it would be grossly unfair to portray William Sanday as a mere historicist, since he came increasingly to stress the creative aspect within the Gospels (cf. Sanday [1920]). Of course, there are also passages which are difficult to explain on the assumption of Markan priority, but an informed choice between the two options can only be arrived at by considering the strengths and weaknesses of each point of view; precisely that has been the program of research, grounded in the axiom of the generation of document from document.

In the second half of his book, Farmer presents his defence of Griesbach's solution. In addition to arguing it is a satisfactory account of the evidence which is to be explained, Farmer insists it is manifestly more logical that Streeter's solution. His claim rests on the observation that theories such as Streeter's are inadequate because they involve the postulation of hypothetical documents prior to the Gospels. As we have already seen, there are difficulties in making any firm statements about sources of this kind, and the multiplication of them is likely to make the approach as a whole seem arbitrary. The recognition of these problems brought Farmer to the conclusion that accounts of the Synoptic relationship are to be preferred which involve the supposition that one Gospel was the source of another, that there is directly literary dependence. In support of his programmatic preference, Farmer insisted that it is wrong to hypothesize documents which no longer exist on the grounds that, in logic, the number of entities should not be increased unless it is necessary to increase them. This rule, commonly known as Occam's razor after William of Occam, lies at the heart of Farmer's analysis; once he invokes it against solutions that involve hypothetical documents, he has only to deal with theories which posit direct dependence among the Gospels. Variants of these include the solution of Austin Farrer (1954, 1955), according to whom Mark was the first Evangelist, Matthew the second and Luke the third, and of B. C. Butler, who simply argued that the order of the canon is the order of the sources. Among the solutions of a directly literary relationship, there is also that of Michael Goulder (1978) and that of John Drury (1976):

rather than taking Mark as a synopsis of Matthew and Luke, they argue that Luke is a synopsis of Matthew and Mark. Even if Farmer is correct in preferring such theories, therefore, there remain many contenders with which Griesbach's hypothesis must compete.

More fundamentally, Farmer's application of Occam's razor is itself to be questioned on logical grounds. William of Occam developed his rule in order to promote clarity in philosophical thought. In his time, the argument was current that because a word exists, there must be an actual and distinct reality which corresponds to that word. Occam's rule was devised to guard against that inference, and to insist that some evidential support is necessary in order to assert that anything exists. "Virtue," for example, cannot be assumed to exist as an entity in itself, apart from people who are virtuous. Farmer does not apply the rule to the realm of philosophy, but to the realm of history: in making this transition, he does not seem to be aware he is misconstruing Occam. As a principle in philosophy, the razor casts doubt on the assumption of philosophical entities for which there is no evidence. But once the existence of such an entity is granted, the razor cannot determine how many things belong to the entity. For example, "humanity" is an entity of philosophy; the population of the earth is not. In other words, a single entity in philosophy is not the same as a single thing in our experience: a philosophical entity is a category to which one, or several, or many things might belong. Turning to the issue at hand, we can say that the existence of the category "documents" is agreed on all sides; the question is whether one may properly hypothesize documents such as "Q". In logic, there is no reason why not: the entity of "document" is still in view. The historical dispute concerns how many documents, and of what sort. One's decision about "Q" must rest on an evaluation of the plausibility that such a document might have existed, and of its adequacy as an account of the Synoptic relationship. There is not a philosophical short cut which obviates consideration of this kind; by arguing that there is a logical way of excluding Streeter's theory, Farmer

himself added his own fallacy to the history of
discussion.

   What Farmer has successfully uncovered, however,
is the radical tendency of Sanday's seminar to think
in terms of documents, or of nothing at all. Sanday
himself differed from the view that the form of Mark
known to Luke was an "Ur-Marcus" ([1911] x, xi, xv, 3,
21), disagreed with John C. Hawkins's appeal to oral
tradition in order to account for variants from Mark
in the Lukan passion ([1911] xiii, xiv), and sided
with Hawkins in the description of "Q" as an actual
document ([1911] xiv, xi, xix, xx, 3). The rationale
of Sanday's position does not lie only in his
adjudication among competing theories of Synoptic
development. His position is succinctly represented in
his essay in *Studies* ([1911] 1-26). In a brief
prolegomenon, which is so lucid as still to merit
careful reading, Sanday explains that the essential
challenge posed by "the Synoptic Problem" is to hit
upon a theory which accounts for both resemblances and
variations among the Synoptic Gospels. He then
distinguishes the alternatives which strike his mind
as evident:

> Now, just as it is the strong point of the
> documentary theory to account for agreements, so
> it is the strong point of the oral theory to
> account for differences ([1911] 5).

He further acknowledges that the latter "are of such a
kind as to suggest oral tradition" as a natural
explanation. Nonetheless, Sanday operates under what
he self-consciously assumes is the hypothesis (and
only that) of Markan priority and literary dependence
among the Synoptic Gospels, and the program of his
article (and of his seminar generally) was to test and
refine that assumption as evidence was investigated.
Notably, neither he nor any of his colleagues appears
to have speculated on the shape a comprehensively oral
theory might take.

   Operating within his stated assumption, then,
Sanday proceeds to describe what he calls the
"psychological" and "external" conditions under which

the "Evangelists" as a whole functioned. Under the category of "psychological conditions," Sanday had in mind what we would today call the intention of the "Evangelists." He describes them as "historians," rather than "copyists" ([1911] 12): they did not have access to the best authorities, and in part their aim was homiletic (pp. 13-16), but they did intend to render their essentially reliable sources faithfully. Sanday further qualifies his description of the "Evangelists" as historians by reference to the physical conditions under which they worked. He suggests that those features of the Gospels which "simulate oral transmission" (p. 19) were in fact produced by the exigencies of copying in antiquity, in which one "would probably read through a whole paragraph (*sic!*) at once, and trust to his memory to convey the substance of it safely from one book to another" (p. 18).

Whatever might be said of the particulars of Sanday's portrait of Synoptic development, the outstanding feature of his approach is its synthesis of disparate elements, each of which had been considered as a matter worthy of attention in itself. He was, therefore, no mere conduit of Holtzmann's hypothesis, but a careful and at the same time creative recipient, who considered technical data within a horizon of historical probabilities. Once one has said that, however, Sanday's extraordinary provincialism remains: he simply omitted to consider the work of his great, somewhat older contemporary at Cambridge, Brooke Foss Westcott. In a profoundly influential work (which went through many editions), *Introduction to the Study of the Gospels* (1860), Westcott had argued for the relative independence of the Gospels, against theories of literary dependence, by reference to "the successive remoulding of the oral Gospel according to the peculiar requirements of different classes of hearers" ([1896] 214). In other words, Westcott dispensed with any axiom of the purely documentary generation of documents, and appealed to oral, apostolic tradition and social forces in order to explain the relationship among the first three Gospels ([1896] 174-253).

Although Sanday's seminar was constituted to address Holtzmann's hypothesis in particular, and to that extent was absolved from treating of other theses, the fact is that oral tradition was appealed to time and again by the participants, in order to account for otherwise inexplicable deviations of one "document" from another. Instances of the appeal to oral tradition have already been cited in the case of Hawkins's work, but B. H. Streeter -- without doubt the most prominent member of the seminar, and the greatest contributor to "the Synoptic Problem" of this century -- represents the problem best of all. Streeter's contributions to the volume edited by Sanday, as the final communication of the seminar, focus on the hypothetical document called "Q." Streeter concluded that the order of the document is better preserved in Luke than in Matthew, and that the latter has carved the document up to serve the literary structure of five discourses of Jesus ([1911] 151, 157-158). He also came quite firmly to the conclusion that Mark also knew the source "Q" in writing (pp. 165-166, 176-177), and a reluctant Sanday came around to that point of view ([1911] xvi). Because Streeter considered "Q" a written source, probably "of an original (*sic!*) eyewitness" (p. 185, cf. p. 216), the delineation of the document appeared important to him. On the supposition that "Q" would have been treated by the "Evangelists" much as Matthew and Luke treated Mark (p. 185), he argued that the matter peculiar to the later Gospels might originally have been contained in "Q" (p. 184). He offered Luke 9:51-15:10 and 17:1-18:8 as "highly speculative" candidates for inclusion in "Q" (p. 206).

The reason for Streeter's consuming interest in "Q" becomes plainest in "The Literary Evolution of the Gospels" ([1911] 210-231), which Sanday himself commended as a sound and scientific conspectus "of the whole course of development in the Apostolic and sub-Apostolic age in its bearing upon literary composition in general and the composition of the Gospels in particular" (p. xvi). Streeter argues that, in the initial phase of development, "*only that was written down which one would be likely to forget*," and that "Q is perfectly intelligible as a document written *to supplement* the living tradition of a generation which had known Christ" (p. 215). Mark, on the other hand, "wrote to *supplement* Q," which is why his Gospel so often "mentions Jesus' teaching without citing it" (p. 219). Matthew and Luke were quite distinctive in their purposes, being written with an "aim of completeness" (p. 200), the former in terms of a discursive account of Jesus' teaching (p. 222), the latter in terms of inspirational biography (pp. 222-223).

Streeter's greatest work, *The Four Gospels* (1924), well represents the concern with development which Sanday had so warmly recommended. He builds upon the work of Westcott and Hort in order to construe the ancient manuscripts of the New Testament as witness to the geographical variety among early Christians. His account of how variants arose, and were later homogenized, remains illuminating, and his designations of major groups of variants, as Alexandrian, Western, Caesarean, and Byzantine, continue to be used. Analysis by locality also characterizes Streeter's approach to the canonical Gospels. Building upon his essays in *Studies*, Streeter sketched "The Fundamental Solution" of the Synoptic interrelationship in a single chapter ([1924] 149-198): Mark is located at Rome (c. A. D. 60), "Q" at Antioch (c. A. D. 50), Matthew at Antioch (c. A. D. 85), and Luke at Corinth (c. A. D. 80).

In certain crucial respects, Streeter's presentation of 1924 considerable refines the picture he offered in 1911. The Gospel according to Mark is now viewed as "taken down from rapid dictation by word of mouth" (p. 163): the relation to "Q" is more attenuated than Streeter had earlier indicated it was. That Mark is stylistically more primitive than Matthew and Luke is to Streeter's mind irrefutable (p. 164), and the distribution of Markan matter in the later Gospels seems to him "only explicable on the theory that each author had before him the Marcan material already embodied in one single document" (p. 165). In contrast to this increased confidence in Markan priority, Streeter in 1924 is far more ambivalent as

to "Q" than he was in 1911. He is not now certain it
was a written document (p. 184, cf. p. 237), and
insists that efforts to specify the precise contents
of "Q" -- including his own -- are fruitless (p. 185,
cf. pp., 239-242). Increasingly, Streeter thinks in
terms of cycles of tradition, rathen than in terms of
documentary dependence. While in 1911 Mark is
described as using his memory of "Q," by 1924 Streeter
describes Mark and "Q" as "overlapping:" "to put it
paradoxically, the overlapping of Mark and Q is more
certain than the existence of Q" (p. 186). The actual
difficulty, however, is not so much the existence as
the definition of "Q:" if it is not quite a document,
and "overlaps," rather than supplies Mark, what sort
of entity is it?

What Streeter offers to explain himself is an
analogy. He had collaborated with A. J. Appasamy in a
work on the Indian mystic, Sadhu Sundar Singh (1921).
In the process of that work, he discovered the
phenomenon of overlapping written and oral sources,
and compared his own work on Sadhu to that of the
"Evangelists" ([1924] 192-195). In a piece on
"Proto-Luke" ([1924] 199-222), Streeter argues that,
prior to Luke, "Q" had been combined with matter
pecular to Luke, thus reversing his stand of 1911, in
which the virtual integrity of "Q" within Luke had
been argued. By the time one reads "A Four Document
Hypothesis" (pp. 223-279), "Q" is also held to overlap
with "M," material peculiar to Matthew (pp. 251-252).
Streeter has been faulted in recent discussion chiefly
for his acceptance of Markan priority (cf. Farmer
[1976] 118-177); but when his analysis is taken within
its own terms of reference, his understanding of what
constitutes a document appears to be the primary
difficulty.

If the sources posited by Streeter appear
defective as documents, it is perhaps an even more
telling criticism of his approach to remark that the
Gospels which are held to be a function of those
sources also appear less than coherent. In his
presentation of "A Four Document Hypothesis," Streeter
(1924) argues his case by taking the example of the
parable of the mustard seed (Matthew 13:31-32; Mark

4:30-32;   Luke   13:18-19).   The   three   versions   are
explained (pp. 246-248) by the supposition that Mark's
text has been used by Matthew, who conflated Mark and
"Q." "Q," on the other hand, is held to be represented
by Luke's version of the parable. Streeter bases his
case on the observation that of the 31 words that
appear in Matthew (omitting "and," the verb "to be,"
the definite article and pronouns), only seven are
peculiar by comparision to Mark and Luke. Another
seven appear in Mark and Luke, ten are found in Mark
alone, and seven in Luke alone. Streeter also sets out
the three Greek texts and designates their agreements.

By following Streeter's table, we can trace the
editorial process which Matthew is alleged to reflect.
The initial statement is, "He set another parable
before them, saying..." (Matthew 13:31a.) The term
"parable" does not appear in Luke, but it is present
at the end of Jesus' statement in Mark (4:30: "How
shall we liken the kingdom of God, or in what parable
should we put it?"). The placement of the word is
therefore different, and its case is not the same
(being dative in Mark, accusative in Matthew), but
Streeter supposes direct dependence here. Matthew next
introduces the words of the parable, "The kingdom of
the heavens is like to a mustard seed, which a man
takes and sows in his field" (13:31b,c). The words "is
like" and "which a man takes" appear in exactly the
same form in Luke (13:18b, c-13:19a), but not in Mark.
"His field" in Matthew corresponds to "his own garden"
in Luke; Mark again has no such reference. But, on
Streeter's analysis, Matthew is not consistently
following "Q" even in this half verse, in that a form
of the verb "to sow" appears in Mark, but not in Luke.
In other words, Matthew is drawing "from one or
another of his two sources" throughout, as Streeter
says (p. 247).

The striking feature of the alleged conflation
is its apparent lack of discrimination among the two
sources: at any given moment, Matthew might be using
Mark, "Q," or both. The situation is the same in
respect of the next verse in Matthew according to
Streeter. The mustard is "the smallest of all seeds,
but when it grows it is greatest of all herbs, and

becomes a tree, so that the birds of the air come and dwell in its branches" (Matthew 13:32). The terms "smallest," "of all seeds," "when," "becomes," "greatest," "of all herbs," and "so that" are shared with Mark alone (4:31b-32). In addition, the verb "to dwell" appears in the infinitive rather than in the indicative, singular (as Luke has it). The verb "to grow," the word "tree" and the phrase "in its branches" are shared with Luke alone (13:19b). On the whole, then, Streeter paints a consistent picture of Matthew's editorial activity.

The question which emerges when we consider Streeter's suggestion is whether, even granting that we can see the texts as related in the way proposed, we arrive at a coherent and satisfying account of the development of the Gospels and their present meaning when we do so. Streeter's picture of Matthew requires us to see him as a highly conservative editor who is reserved in using his own words. Within the limits of the example, this portrait is satisfactory, although we might perhaps find it difficult to conceive of Matthew flipping back and forth between two source documents. Does he, for example, seated on the ground in the manner of ancient scribes, have Mark and "Q" opened on either side of him as he writes on a third scroll? Does he pick up Mark, read, write a few words, put it down and then turn to Luke? Or does he have assistants who read bits of the sources out to him?

If the latter picture seems a bit easier to imagine, what evidence have we that Christians during this period had the material and human resources available to mount such an operation? By the fourth century, such a process would certainly be possible: indeed, codices of the New Testament were then produced by reading from an exemplar to a group of scribes, and the reader might then check the scribal copies against his original. For such an operation, the production of Matthew from Mark and "Q" would require much more organized and demanding activity, but it would not be impossible. But the Church of the first century did not enjoy the official toleration and financial support which came under Constantine, and there is no mention in the New Testament of a settled scriptorium. There are, indeed, mentions of ink and papyrus (cf. 2 John 12), but no references to the professional production of scrolls. Again, even Paul appears to have used amanuenses (cf. Romans 16:22), who wrote from dictation, but such functionaries did not apparently collate documents and harmonize them. Perhaps, therefore, it is better to think of Streeter's Matthew as working more on his own, given a junior assistant of the sort Paul used. Nonetheless, we must still imagine that he had access to something in the order of a Christian library.

As Matthew conflated Mark and "Q," he would, on Streeter's reading, have had recourse to yet other sources, above all "M," a "cycle of tradition of a distinctly Judaistic bias" (p. 260). We must add these sources to Matthew's library, and therefore to the operating budget we imagine he had. Immediately prior to the parable of the mustard seed, Matthew has the parable of the tares (13:24-30). It is uniquely Matthean, and Streeter's analysis would assign it to "M," although it does not appear in his index. Curiously, this uniquely Matthean parable begins with exactly the same words which introduce the parable of the mustard seed: "He set another parable before them, saying..." Obviously, Matthew did not derive these words from Mark, so that there is no reason to follow Streeter in thinking that he did so later. Moreover, Matthew's parable of the tares takes the place of the parable of the man, the seed, and the earth in Mark (4:26-29). There are indeed verbal similarities in the two parables of growth, but they are manifestly different in their present form: Matthew's parable deals with the problem of evil, while Mark's speaks of the revelation of the kingdom. Why would Matthew slavishly follow Mark's wording in one parable, and in another case delete a vivid Markan parable altogether? Basically, then, two incongruities emerge as we consider Streeter's analysis. On the one hand, an allegedly Markan word ("parable") is found to be used by Matthew in non-Markan material in the immediate vicinity of the parable of the mustard seed. On the other hand, Matthew is quite prepared to drop Markan material completely. Both difficulties stand out

clearly has soon as we consider the most immediate
context of the parable of the mustard seed, which
Streeter did not attend to.

Similar problems become apparent as we look at
the material which immediately follows the parable of
the mustard seed in Matthew. Matthew 13:33, the
parable of the leaven, parallels Luke 13:20-21, and as
such is to be assigned to "Q" within Streeter's
scheme. It opens with an introduction which by now has
a familiar ring ("He spoke another parable to them,"
cf. 13:24, 31). Again, as Streeter would have it,
Matthew has used non-Markan material and incorporated
a Markan word. He appears more and more to be an
editor of endless ingenuity, and practically no
policy. In vv. 34-35, he returns to Markan material in
speaking of Jesus' general practice of speaking in
parables (cf. Mark 4:33-34), although he adds a
formulaic citation of his own. But a long run of
material follows, comprised of the interpretation of
the parable of the tares, the parable of the treasure,
the parable of the pearl, the parable of the dragnet,
and the saying about every scribe trained for the
kingdom (vv. 36-52), which is for the most part unique
to the first Gospel.

Described in purely mechanical terms, as a
conflation of disparate sources, Matthew 13:24-52
appears rather haphazard. But taken as a whole, this
passage is in fact quite coherent. The parable of the
wheat and the tares (vv. 24-30) is introduced as
"another parable" (v. 24) immediately after the
parable of the sower and its interpretation (vv.
1-23). What reason is there for this ordering? There
is apparent in Matthew, within the discussion that
intervenes between the parable of the sower and its
interpretaion, an emphasis on understanding parabolic
discourse as a whole. The disciples ask Jesus (v. 10):
"Why do you speak in parables?" Jesus answers by
saying the parables disclose the kingdom to his
disciples (v.11), and this amounts to a peculiar
addition to what they already have (v. 12). Others
simply fail to see, hear and understand (v. 13), but
the disciples are blessed, because they see and hear
what even the prophets and righteous men desired to

see and hear, but did not (vv. 16-17). The form of the initial question in Matthew is unique: only here do the disciples ask about the reason for parabolic discourse as a whole. Likewise, the Matthean placement of v. 12 and vv. 16-17 is unique, so that the emphasis on the peculiar understanding of the disciples is obvious. Even in the interpretation of the parable of the sower, this emphasis comes to expression, in that those who are by the wayside are here uniquely identified as people who hear the word of the kingdom and do not understand (v. 19). The issue of such understanding is therefore crucial to an appreciation of the parable of the sower (including its interpretation) in Matthew, and may be taken to be of some importance in the parable of the wheat and the tares.

In fact, it emerges that the latter parable is presented in much the same was that the sower is. Vv. 24-30 give the parable itself, while the interpretation apears in vv. 36-43, and a brief statement about Jesus' habit of speaking in parables intervenes (vv. 34-35). Structurally, this repeats the pattern in vv. 1-23, but it also offers a more precise account of the "word of the kingdom" (v. 19) which the disciples are to understand. In the interpretation of the parable of wheat and tares, the kingdom belongs to the son of man (v. 41), not God, and his rule is openly established at the end of time (v. 40) as he metes out punishment (v. 42) and reward (v. 43). In other words, Jesus in Matthew begins to speak of God's kingdom using the imagery of ordinary experience (sower, planting, weeds, etc.), but then offers the private understanding that he speaks of apocalyptic events associated with the son of man's kingdom which only the disciples are in a position to appreciate.

Sandwiched between the parable and its interpretation, and preceding the general reference to Jesus' parabolic discourse (vv. 34-35), which echoes the earlier statement of the purpose of the parables (vv. 11-15), the parables of the mustard seed and the leaven appear. Both are introduced under the rubric of "another parable" (vv. 31, 33) which was first used in v. 24 to introduce the wheat and the tares. The reader is therefore led to see the wheat and the tares as a continuation of the teaching which the sower is designed to convey, and the two shorter parables as briefer examples of the same sort of material. The wheat and the tares therefore emerge as the center of Jesus' parables in Matthew, because it provides the clear understanding of the kingdom to which the sower only alludes, and it is used to bracket the mustard seed and the leaven in such a way that we are led to see them as hinting at the apocalyptic regime of the son of man. The parable of the fish-net in vv. 47-50 is also presented with an explicitly apocalyptic interpretation (vv. 49-50), and this serves to incline the reader to see the parables of the treasure and the pearl in a similar way (vv. 44-45). The consistent policy is therefore apparent: parables of the kingdom which might be seen to express the immanence of the kingdom, the mustard seed, the leaven, the treasure, and the pearl, are bracketed by unequivocally apocalyptic parables (the wheat and the tares with its interpretation, and the fish-net with its).

Far from being a purely mechanical collation, therefore, the parables in Matthew 13 appear to reflect a deliberate program. A message or argument is conveyed by what we read. The parables of Jesus are presented to us as descriptions of the end time, when the son of man will punish the wicked and reward the just. As soon as this is recognized, the structure of Matthew 13 becomes apparent as an instrument of meaning, not a collational accident.

The difficulty with Streeter's hypothesis is that the "Evangelist" is portrayed as so busy juggling literary sources that it is not easy to imagine him as framing a conscious theme at the same time. Of course, it is not impossible that both activities were going on simultaneously, but it must be stressed that in Matthew 13 the meaning of the text is conveyed by its unique order, not merely by the supposed additions to Mark. Indeed, if Matthew's primary purpose is seen as supplementing Mark, the importance of the wheat and the tares as the center of his argument is missed. The most serious failure of Streeter's hypothesis (and of Farmer's) is that it fails to treat the Gospels as coherent documents in themselves. The meaning of each Gospel is ignored in order to explain it as a collation of its sources. We cannot prove that a mechanical procedure of this kind was not followed, but we can say that the meaning of Matthew 13 is not arrived at on the supposition that it was followed. By comparing and contrasting Matthew with Mark and Luke, the peculiar message of the Matthean parables does become evident. But when source-analysis leads us to explain Matthew as a hybrid of Mark and "Q", we are treating the first Gospel as a mere specimen of language rather than as an instrument of meaning. We do not thereby appreciate the meaning of Matthew; rather, we reduce the Gospel to its hypothetically common denominators. That is, even if Streeter has told us something valuable about parts of Matthew, he has not treated of the whole. Meaning has become the victim of analysis.

The failure of Sanday and his colleagues to engage Westcott's work directly and seriously proved fateful. It resulted in "oral tradition" being smuggled in, without a formal examination of that category, in order to paper over difficulties in a purely documentary solution. Treatments of the Synoptics along oral lines have appeared during this century, of course, but they have largely been diverted from a consistent address of the literary relationship amongst the Gospels by an agenda of denying or asserting the historicity of the texts.

Rudolf Bultmann (1921, 1968), building upon the work of K. L. Schmidt (1919) and Martin Dibelius (1919, 1935), portrayed the oral tradition out of which the Gospel emerged as discrete pericopae, susceptible of any order which an editor might like to impose upon them. Controversy has centered more on Bultmann's postulation of the early Church as a place where sayings of and stories about Jesus could be created, rather than on the supposition that the pericopae were neatly arranged into Mark and "Q" prior to the redaction of Matthew and Luke. Indeed, a notable work by Thorleif Boman (1967) had to wait thirty years for publication, although it directly challenges Bultmann's characterization of the oral tradition. Boman was able to show that even illiterate folk traditions from various periods (not to speak of learned, rabbinic discourses) suggest that the picture of isolated units is untenable. Rather, we have to think of developing streams of tradition with an internal logic of their own. Similar findings, in respect of ancient tradition more generally, have been offered within a volume edited by William O. Walker (1975). Such work questions the axiom of the generation of document from document in the study of the Synoptics.

Birger Gerhardsson, in a book called *Memory and Manuscript* (1961), has also challenged Bultmann's model, on two grounds. First, he shows that in the Judaism of Jesus' day, teachers were concerned to see to it that their disciples memorized their teaching accurately. If Jesus was a rabbi of that type -- and the New Testament certainly suggests that he was -- then the source of the Gospels might not be the creative Christian community, but Jesus himself. Second, Gerhardsson shows that rabbinic tradition did not consist of isolated units, but progressed as streams of transmission associated with various teachers. Difficulties emerge when one attempts to characterize the traditions of the Gospels strictly as rabbinic, as I have argued elsewhere: it is problematic to characterize the principal character of early Christianity as professionally skilled in either oral transmission or scribal techniques (cf. Chilton [1984] 13-56). The point remains, however, that Bultmann's pericopae are too abstract to constitute even a reasonable hypothesis concerning the traditions prior to the Gospels.

Unfortunately, the contributions of Boman and Gerhardsson have been assessed more as attacks on Bultmann than as indices of a fresh approach to the Synoptics. And there is a tendency in their work, as well as in the recent book by Bo Reicke (1982), to align cycles of oral tradition strictly with apostolic witnesses, with the result that the literary relationship among the Synoptic texts may become lost in disputes concerning the historical reliability of the Gospels. The road not taken in Sanday's seminar is not the dispute over the accuracy of the Gospels: that has been a highway of controversy since the Enlightenment. The road not taken is rather the literary inquiry, whether Westcott's hypothesis of an oral tradition, moulded by the interests of distinct communities, might be tenable.

The great lacuna in Westcott's work is any substantive mention of the literature of early Judaism and rabbinic Judaism. Because that literature instances a complex interplay of oral and scribal transmission, it is an obvious candidate for comparison with the Gospels. Comparison heretofore, in standard volumes such as those of Strack--Billerbeck and Morton Smith, has focussed upon passages whose content appears somewhat analogous to that of passages in the Gospels. In the present volume, five Studies are offered, and the logic of comparison is different. We are concerned, Study by Study, with comparing one set of synoptically related texts to another, and we will permit our categories of analysis to be framed heuristically by that comparison. That is, no assumption of documentary or oral dependence is presupposed. Historical issues can at most interest us marginally. The primary focus is upon comparative synopticity in literary material of varying types: controversy (Study 1), theophany (Study 2), *logia* (Study 3), haggadah (Study 4), and *logia* with haggadah (Study 5). The categorization of that material is not at issue here: it is merely a convenience for commencing with a range of types, in order to determine whether an alternative approach to synopticity in early Judaism and early Christianity is possible.

PART TWO: TEXTUAL STUDIES

YOHANAN BEN ZAKKAI
AND THE DISAPPEARING LEVITES,
JESUS AND THE MISPLACED WIVES

A Rabbi and a Skeptic

Jacob Neusner has isolated a particularly striking puzzle (Neusner [1985] 138), which appears in several rabbinic texts; we consider the version in Bekharoth (5a) first of all:

> Quintroqis asked Yohanan, When Levites are enumerated in detail, you find 22,300. But when counted as a group, 22,000. Where did the 300 go? Three hundred were first-born, and a first-born cannot redeem a first-born (Numbers 3:44).

The scriptural citation within parentheses is provided by Neusner himself, by way of explanation, but further discussion is required to understand the passage.

In Numbers 3:39, the sum of male Levites upwards of one month is put at 22,000. The reference is by no means incidental, but is said to be the result of a formal census instigated at divine command by Moses and Aaron. But 3:39 climaxes a more detailed narrative of the same census in vv. 14-37; the breakdown is by families in that case, and comes to 7,500 from Gershon (3:22), 8,600 from Kohath (3:28), and 6,200 from Merari (3:34). The problem of the missing three hundred Levites is therefore implicit within scripture. Although implicit, the problem is hardly incidental. Within Numbers, the notice of the census totaling 22,000 is followed by notice of a census of the first-born males of Israel from the age of one month and upward (3:40); that count comes to 22,273 (3:43). The actual tallies are held to be important, since a numerical correspondence between the Levites and the Israelite first-born is divinely mandated (vv. 44, 45). The discrepancy of 273 between the number of Israelite first-born is expressly an issue (v. 45) and monetary redemption is mandated as the compensation for the missing numerical redemption by Levites (vv.

46-51).   The   arithmetic   error   therefore   proves
expensive, or lucrative, depending upon one's point of
view.

As we shall see, these intra-scriptural issues
are, to varying degrees, addressed by the haggadoth to
be discussed.   By citing Numbers 3:44 within his
translation, Neusner engages in a style of explanation
at   home   within   the   genre   of   Talmud.   Elucidatory
transmission is necessary to convey the sense of the
haggadah. The difficulty of the vignette, its organic
need of elucidation, is confirmed by the much fuller
version, which also appears as the text of Talmud,
conveyed   by   the   editors   of   the   Soncino   rendering
(Miller and Simon [1948]):

> A Roman general, Controcos, questioned R. Yoḥanan
> ben   Zakkai,   In   the   detailed   record   of   the
> numbering of the Levites, you find the total is
> 22,300, whereas in the sum total you only find
> 22,000. Where are the (remaining) three hundred?
> He replied to him, Three hundred were (Levite)
> first-born,   and   a   first-born   cannot   cancel   the
> holiness of a first-born.

Miller and Simon present their consciously explanatory
glosses within parentheses, but their entire style of
translation   is   considerably   more   expansive   than
Neusner's.   (As a matter of practice, such expansions
upon a text's meaning should be avoided, so as not to
give the impression that there is more variation among
extant   textual   witnesses   than   there   in   fact   is.)
Miller   and   Simon   go   on   to   give   their   explicitly
elucidatory   comments   in   notes.   They   suggest   that
"Controcos" might be Quintus or Quietus, which would
make sense of the association with Yoḥanan, although
-- for that very reason -- the corruption of a
relatively well-known to a perplexing spelling remains
a mystery under their explanation. They also identify
the scriptural sources of the arithmetic confusion.

The   text-critical   decisions,   and   the
explanations offered, by Neusner on the one hand, and
by Miller and Simon on the other, are themselves

instructive. They demonstrate that the desire for explanation which any reader might experience is part and parcel of an intelligent response to the passage, and that such a response influences how the vignette is conveyed. As we shall see, from the moment the Talmudic story was told in writing, it has occasioned scribal elucidation, whether in the form of intra-textual or extra-textual glosses.

In order to avoid being misled by alternative styles of translation in our analysis, a fresh translation of each text considered will be offered. Appendix I provides reference to editions consulted, and gives the original presupposed in our translation, as well as certain statistical observations (whose significance is explained below). Comparison of our appendix with the editions cited will enable the reader to infer the text-critical decisions which have been made, as in the case of Bekharoth 5a:

> Qontroqos, the prince, questioned Rabbi Yohanan ben Zakkai. In the detailed count of Levites, you find 22,000 and 300; in the general count, you find 22,000. So where did three hundred go? He said to him, Those three hundred were first-born, and first-born does not cancel first-born.

The haggadah goes on to cite supporting opinion, and to offer another challenge, with the introduction, "They asked...".

As we consider the story, it becomes plain that the question posed by the Roman general, however he is named, is substantive, even though arithmetic. The number of the Levites as a whole is in fact given as 22,000 in Numbers 3:39. In chapter four of the same book, those between the ages of 30 and 50 years old (the appropriate age-range of those who were to perform cultic service) are numbered. The enumeration is done according to the families of Kohath, Gershon, and Merari, as is commanded by the LORD (4:1-3, 21-23, 29, 30) and the particular duties of each group are laid down. Moses and Aaron then number those qualified of Kohath (at 2,750, Numbers 4:34-37), Gershon (at

2,630, Numbers 4:38-41), and Merari (at 3,200, Numbers 4:42-45). The resultant number of 8,580 qualified persons is correctly given (4:46-48). In v. 49, it is stressed that the appointed service and the enumeration were both completed by Moses at the LORD's command. The structure of the passage corresponds to such a dual emphasis upon appointment and enumeration. In the case of each group, the LORD commands the count, and then specifies the sort of service envisaged; the accomplishment of the census by Moses and Aaron, in the same order of the divine command, is then detailed. There can be no question, therefore, but that arithmetic -- within scripture itself -- is implicitly crucial.

The observation of numerical stress in chapter 4 in two respects confirms our observation of the difficulty in chapter 3. First, the population envisaged in the census of the earlier chapter, males from one month and upward, is viewed very differently from those specified in chapter 4; indeed, the difference is as great as the distinction between the logic of redemption and that of cultic service. The count in chapter 3 concerns those who belong to the LORD, while in chapter 4 the important, but by no means more crucial, issue is that of the performance of cultic tasks. Second, chapter 4 demonstrates what is in any case obvious, that sums can be tallied correctly; the error implicit in chapter 3 therefore appears all the more egregious.

In the Septuagint, the numerical discrepancy is mitigated, but not resolved. The family of Merari at 3:34 is numbered at 6,050, rather than at 6,200. It may be conjectured that, at an earlier stage (prior to the programmatic accommodation to the Hebrew text in the second century, cf. Barthelémy [1963] 1-160), a reduction in the number of another family by the same amount resolved the problem neatly and completely. Approximating such economical means of harmonization, a modern interpreter might suggest that textual corruption is the culprit (as in the case of J. Marsh [1953] 155), and appeal to hypothetical sources or redactions when that fails, but such expedients are not to be found amongst the rabbinic solutions here surveyed.

The false sum of Numbers 3:39, then, becomes the basis of a problem: Moses numbers the first-born of Israel, whom the Levites are supposed to redeem, at 22,273 (3:43). A correct tallying of the sum of the Levites would have meant there was too much redemption, not too little, but the text goes on to require money of redemption, at five shekels a head, for the allegedly unredeemed Israelites (3:44-51), or 1,365 shekels. The arithmetic disappearance of 300 Levites, then, is of economic import, and puts in question the numeracy of the passage as a whole, on which a taxing edifice is built.

The mocking question to put Yoḥanan is astute and subtle, not only numerate, and demands a response if the integrity of scripture is to be maintained (which is the unstated program behind any attempt to grapple with the question). It may fairly be doubted whether a Roman general was as much in touch with the arithmetic of scripture as the question presupposes, and even whether the rabbis who told the story expected their identification of the interlocutor to be credited. Levitical regulations were a rabbinic, not a Roman, passion (cf. Neusner [1981] 217-229). More probably, a question arose within rabbinic discussion, in the idiom of numerical debate, and was imputed to a Gentile skeptic, once the doubt it represented was held to be inappropriate. It is notable that the preceding section of Bekharoth (4b-5a) consists of a long dispute between Yoḥanan and Resh Laqish concerning the sanctification of the first-born in the wilderness. Moreover, the passage itself continues with a reference to what "they" asked, as if "Qontroqos" were not the only person at issue. Yoḥanan was reputed to have had contacts with generals, and his legendarily great age (of 120 years in all; cf. Neusner [1985] 136-138) would theoretically have permitted him contact with Quietus, a notoriously anti-Jewish figure (cf. Stemberger [1983] 76-78). Yoḥanan is simple and direct, in keeping with his normal response to Gentile skepticism in various haggadoth: because three hundred of the Levites were themselves first-born, they could not redeem those of Israel who were first-born. The initial question is treated as sophomoric: the interlocutor can count, but he does not understand redemption. Those implications are not spelled out, but the rhetoric of the passage within the circle of tradition associated with Yoḥanan invites the reader or hearer to draw such conclusions. Other conclusions, drawn from a reading of Numbers three, are not invited: the integrity of scripture is defended in cultic terms, and its bad arithmetic is simply covered up under a shroud of contempt for generals.

A passage in the Talmud Yerushalmi is obviously comparable to what we read in Babli (see Neusner [1985] 138 and Appendix I), and yet frustratingly different:

> Antoninut the ruler questioned Rabbi Yoḥanan ben Zakkai, In general they are lacking, and in particular they exceed. He said to him, Those three hundred who exceed were the first-born of the priesthood, and holy cannot discharge holy.

As presented here, the Gentile questioner is both more astute than "Qontroqos" (as he should be, given his promotion), and less prosaic. "In general they are lacking," he laconically remarks; the sum in Numbers 3:39 falls short of the number of Israelite first-born (3:43). But "in particular they exceed," because the actual total of those of Gershon, Kohath, and Merari exceeds the 22,273 of the Israelites. Yoḥanan's answer is more sententious than it is in Babli, "holy cannot discharge holy." The pretension of the questioner is put firmly in its place, by Yoḥanan's insistence that the issue is cultic, not numerical.

The version of the story in Yerushalmi is so abbreviated and paradoxical as to be cryptic. Neusner styles it as "garbled" ([1985] p.139), and some fuller knowledge of the entire question on the reader's part must be presupposed for the point of the question, and of the answer, to be appreciable. That "Antoninut," a ruler, is now at issue heightens the sense of the question as stereotyped: the presumable reference is to Antoninus Pius, who is usually placed in haggadic conversation, not with Yoḥanan, but with Yehuda ha-Nasi (cf. Stemberger [1983] 86-94). The form of the question, for all that it is obscure, is now entirely numerical. By the same token, there is even less room here than there is in Babli to undermine Yoḥanan's claim to authority by looking too closely at the text of Numbers. Interestingly, the discussion is taken up (after the passage cited) by other rabbis, which supports the speculation offered above, in respect of an actually intramural controversy behind Bekharoth 5a. The contextual matter at hand in Yerushalmi is the constitution of the Sanhedrin, and the ideological sense of numbers appears to be the point at issue generally.

In Numbers Rabbah 4:9, still another version of this notable meeting of minds appears (cf. the shorter interpretation in 3:14). In this case, the version is so full as to make the sense of the story unmistakable (cf. Appendix I):

And this was the question Hongetys the ruler posed to Rabbi Yoḥanan ben Zakkai. He said to him, Moses your rabbi was either a thief, or he was not able to reckon. He said to him, Why? Hongetys said to him, Because there were 22,000 first-born, and also 273. And the Place commanded, The Levites redeem in the case of the first-born. Grant that there are 22,000 of the Levites, corresponding to 22,000 among the first-born, and there are still found among the Levites 300 exceeding the 22,000, as was reckoned in the first count, in detail. For what reason did those 300 of the Levites not redeem those 273 first-born, who were above and beyond the 22,000 first-born? Indeed, we find those 273 each giving five shekels. Further, for what reason, when he tallies the number of the Levites at the end, does he deduct 300 of them from the first count? Did he not steal them from the reckoning, so that

those 273 first-born might each give five shekels
to Aaron his brother? Or was he, perchance,
unable to reckon? Rabbi Yoḥanan said to him, He
was not a thief and he knew how to reckon, but
one word whispers to me, speaking to you. He said
to him, Speak. Rabbi Yoḥanan ben Zakkai said to
him, You know how to read, but you are not able
to interpret. He said, Those 22,000 belonging to
the Levites redeem 22,000 belonging to the
first-born. There still remained among the
Levites 300, among the first-born still 273.
Those 300 which were among the Levites were
first-born, and first-born does not redeem
first-born. Therefore he rounds off those put
aside, because they were first-born. Immediately
he parted from him.

Numbers Rabbah presents the fullest "account" of
Yoḥanan's argument with a Gentile interlocutor, this
time a ruler named Hongetys. The new skeptic is the
most loquacious we have encountered, and he puts his
charge in the most telling form, in that Moses is
charged with fraud and/or innumeracy. On the other
hand, Hongetys is set up for a fall, in that Numbers
Rabbah 3:14 (and the first half of 4:9) provides the
solution of the exegetical riddle in advance of his
question. The relevance of Numbers 3:45-51 is
explicitly acknowledged within the haggadah, and the
story is rounded out in order to vindicate Moses
against both of the charges against him. Notably, that
is only possible by computing from an axis of
redemption, rather than from a count of heads. Within
the logic of redemption, the total number of
Israelites and Levites is not an issue, once the
persons concerned are first-born. Neither the 300
Levites nor the 273 Israelites are at issue, owing to
their status, not their number. On the axis of
redemption, they must be counted in some other way.
What "Hongetys" had failed to see (for the simple
reason no hint of it is to be found in the Hebrew
text) was that the 300 "extra" Levites just happened
to be first-born, and so were dropped from the

redemptive computation. Hongetys is expressly made to play the fool in Numbers Rabbah, since -- as we have seen -- an extensive explanation of the scriptural issues (much as has been offered at the start of the present discussion) precedes his observation.

Synopsis

Within the study of the Gospels, there is an assumption which has been invoked from time to time, known as "historicism" (cf. R. T. France [1971]). It applies to the judgment of the historical accuracy of texts the criterion of Anglo-Saxon jurisprudence, that one is innocent until one is proven guilty. In other words, historical accuracy is equated with legal innocence, and interpretative creativity with legal guilt; unless positive evidence suggests the latter is more plausible, the former is presumed. In two of its presuppositions, historicism must be regarded as an unworthy instrument of research: (1) it imputes to ancient texts the historical prejudices of one sector of modern consciousness, and (2) it implies there is adequate evidence to hand to falsify every inaccuracy in the Gospels. The first presupposition, the imputation of a modern desire for historical accuracy to the Gospels, is falsified by the Synoptic relationship itself, which could not exist had imaginative interpretation of some order not been encouraged. The second presupposition, of adequate data to discover inaccuracies, founders upon the social reality that Jesus' movement and Christianity were not sufficiently important in their earliest stages to attract either support or refutation from contemporary historians. In the present case, operating under the supposition of historicism would lead one to the conclusion that Yoḥanan on three separate occasions engaged Gentile officials (Qontroqos, Antoninus, and Hongetys), in a debate concerning the accounting of Levitical redemption in Numbers 3, 4. If the plausibility of such a reconstruction is strained from the point of view of Yoḥanan's usual sphere of interest, a greater

inconvenience is that such an understanding of the
facts behind the stories would require a significant
alteration in descriptions of Roman policy in the
provinces. A postulation of active, Imperial interest
in self-evidently religious matters simply runs
against the grain of the available evidence. To
suppose that we are given three versions of the same
story in Babli, Yerushalmi, and Midrash Rabbah, seems
rather more economical, to say the very least.

    Of the three versions, the one in Numbers Rabbah
is the best formed; it is virtually self-explanatory,
and conflates the underlying issues, of the general
and the specific computations of the numbers of the
Israelites and Levites and of the tax of five shekels,
into a single discourse. But we have no way of knowing
whether separated questions such as we might read in
Babli and Yerushalmi were the basis on which the
passage in Midrash Rabbah was composed. Likewise,
Yerushalmi presupposes the reader's awareness of the
issue involved, but it does not necessarily assume
knowledge of Babli (or of Numbers Rabbah) in
particular. Babli casts the story within the early
period of Judaism, when Yoḥanan had to deal with
generals, rather than rulers, but that by no means
guarantees that its version of the story is in fact
the earliest. In fact, its omission explicitly to cope
with the question of the numerical excess of Levites
over Israelites in Numbers 3 (cf. Yerushalmi and
Midrash Rabbah) leaves Yoḥanan's answer looking
partial, and open to some logical doubt.

    The particular contours and distinctive
contributions of each version are evident. Babli is
relatively straightforward, and contexted in
potentially military confrontation; Yerushalmi is
cryptic, and imagines a settled, gnomic opposition;
Midrash Rabbah is comprehensive, and presents an
almost erudite skepticism. Such characterizations of
the texts are possible by reading each version in
respect of the others. They demand such a reading.
They not only relate substantially the same story: the
elements within them are comparable, and their diction
may be collated. Yerushalmi and Numbers Rabbah agree

that the interlocutor is a ruler, and have him charge
that Moses was either a thief or innumerate. Babli and
Numbers Rabbah agree that the Levites were counted "in
detail," and that "first-born cannot redeem
first-born." The particular silhouette of each story
interfaces with the others, and yet is distinctive.

The literary interrelationship of these stories
constitutes a field within which each can be
appreciated. Three distinctive rhetorical programs are
executed, and different sorts of imaginary opponents
are overcome. But their interrelationship presents
itself as a factor of comparative reading, not as an
account of how the texts came to be as they are. That
one passage was worked up scribally from another, or
others, cannot be proved in this case (so Neusner
[1985] 139, 140); but for the possibility of analogy
to the Synoptic Gospels, such a reconstruction would
probably not even be attempted. The three documents as
a whole, Babli, Yerushalmi, and Midrash Rabbah, are
far too idiosyncratic for a scribal theory to be
applied globally. Moreover, chronological
considerations have made such an approach appear
impracticable: Babli is widely dated to around A. D.
500, Yerushalmi c. A. D. 400, and Numbers Rabbah no
earlier than the twelfth century.

Relatively to one another, however, the three
stories represent how a common tradition can be told
more or less plainly, more or less economically, and
more or less comprehensively. Explication,
abbreviation, and intercalation are manifest as we
move from Babli, to Yerushalmi, to Midrash Rabbah. As
we do so, we may appreciate the distinctive impact of
each story, but what becomes of Yoḥanan ben Zakkai?
His engagement with the basic question about Numbers
3:39 is taken for granted throughout, but the setting
of the debate is so malleable that it seems not to
have been regarded as basic, even by the storytellers,
as the three versions evolved. Complete agnosticism
about Yoḥanan would be inappropriate; at least, his
association with the issue was a durable feature of
rabbinic memory. But the interrelation of the texts,
in the absence of a viable theory of dependence

(scribal or oral), militates against taking any one of them as factual in its present form.

Jesus and the Question of Divorce

In the presentation of Jesus' teaching of divorce within the Synoptic Gospels, we are presented with formations (or deformations) of tradition which are comparable to the instances we have just considered. In the case of Rabbi Jesus, as well, expansion, elucidation, intercalation, and radical abbreviation are manifest in the emergence of haggadoth.

The Matthean version reads as follows (19:3-12; again, cf. Appendix I for the texts here presupposed):

> And Pharisees came to him, testing him and saying, Is it fitting to divorce one's wife for any reason? He answered, Have you not read that the one who created from the beginning made them male and female? It says, On account of this a man shall leave father and mother, and adhere to his wife, and the two will be one flesh. So they are no longer two, but one flesh. A man shall not, then, divide what God as paired. They say to him, Then why did Moses command to give a certificate of dissolution, and divorce? He says to them, Moses permitted you to divorce your wives for your hardness of heart, but from the beginning it has not been so. And I say to you that whoever divorces his wife, except for indecency, and marries another, commits adultery. The disciples say to him, If such is the relationship of man with woman, it is not beneficial to marry! But he said to them, Not all accept this precept, but those to whom it has been given. For there are eunuchs who were begotten so from the mother's womb, and eunuchs who were castrated by men, and eunuchs who castrated themselves for the sake of the kingdom of the heavens. He who accepts, should accept!

Matthew's Jesus is confronted by his typical

disputants, the "Pharisees," and they are additionally styled as "testing" him. The antipathy of the question is therefore established (see 16:1; 22:18). In Mishnah (Gittin 9:10), Shammai, Hillel, and Aqiba are said to have pronounced differently on the grounds of divorce implied in Deuteronomy 24:1-4. As is widely commented upon, Jesus' position begins with a view of marriage, developed from Genesis 1:27; 2:24, rather than a specific teaching about divorce. The divine pairing in creation is taken to militate against divorce (19:6). The statement deflects, more than it addresses, the initial question, which asked whether divorce could be undertaken "for any reason" (19:3).

The form of the initial question, which is unique to Matthew, makes sense within the presentation of the Gospel overall. In the "Sermon on the Mount," Jesus has already insisted that "everyone who divorces his wife, apart from a case of indecency, makes her commit adultery, and whoever marries a divorcée commits adultery" (5:32). In context, this statement is expressed in terms of tension with Deuteronomy 24:1-4, in that Matthew 5:31 reads, "And it was said, Whoever divorces his wife should give her a certificate." The question of how Jesus' teaching related to the Hebrew Bible therefore becomes acute, and that question is not, within Matthew, merely a function of "Pharisaic" antipathy.

The acuity of that issue, however, is not such as to imply that Matthew's Jesus in the instance of divorce rejects "the Old Testament" willy-nilly, as is sometimes maintained. Two considerations militate against such a rash conclusion. First, Matthew 5:31, 32 is expressed within the context of hyperbole: it follows the imperative to pluck out one's eye and cut off one's hand at the very hint of adulterous interest (5:27-30). Indeed, the teaching about adultery is doubly hyperbolic in the twin contexts of vv. 27-30 and vv. 31, 32. Physical maiming is spoken of as a response to mere desire (vv. 27-30), and the woman in question is not said to be married, so that the question of actual adultery does not legally arise, as the connection with vv. 31, 32 would imply. Obviously,

5:27-30 is the strongest of disincentives to lust, and
5:31, 32 must be taken as an equally vigorous attack
on divorce. But whether Matthew's readers are actually
to regard all divorce as adultery, and maim themselves
whenever the intention (or intimation) of adultery
arises, remains an open question. Second, our passage
is presented within a section of "the Sermon on the
Mount" known within Christian scholarship as "the
Antitheses." But it is misleading to suppose Jesus'
teaching is logically antithetical to what was taught
formerly within the Matthean presentation. The
"Antitheses" are introduced by the claim that Jesus
came to fulfill the law and the prophets (5:17), and
the continuing validity of the law is expressly
maintained (5:18, 19). A new, abounding righteousness
is said to be required for entry into the kingdom
(5:20), not the rejection of righteousness.

Accordingly, each "antithesis" might more
conveniently be seen as an "extension," intensifying a
scriptural demand, be it in respect of murder
(5:21-26), adultery (5:27-32), swearing (5:33-37),
retaliation (5:38-42), or love (5:43-48). In no case
is the commandment set aside: it generally provides
the occasion for a more stringent demand along similar
lines. Anger is equated with killing, much as desire
is equated with adultery. The saying about divorce
(5:31, 32) is grouped within the section concerning
adultery, with the connective introduction ἐρρέθη δέ.
(Major sections, with breaks of subject, are begun
with the clause, ἠκούσατε ὅτι ἐρρέθη.) The last three
extensions are possessed of a somewhat different
logic. In the cases of swearing and retaliation,
scriptural principles of restraint are pressed to the
point of excluding oaths and revenge completely; in
the case of love, a principle of inclusive love (of
one's "neighbor") is extended without limit. Earlier,
the language of hyperbole had been used: minor
annoyance incurs damnation (5:22), and lust is to be
treated with self-mutilation (5:29, 30). But the last
three extensions employ the logic, rather than merely
the language, of hyperbole, in widening the scope of
what in scripture is a contained admonition. In every

case, however, by language or logic, hyperbole extends
scriptural principles beyond their stated contexts. In
no way is the simplistic abrogation of "the Old
Testament" a part of the rhetorical program.

Particularly, there is a strong indication
within 5:32 that a conscious rejection of Deuteronomy
24:1-4 is not at issue. The exceptive clause, which
speaks of "a case of indecency" (λόγου πορνείας),
corresponds well to the Hebrew of the Mosaic text
concerning divorce, where "a case of indecency" seems
to be the sense of עֶרְוַת דָּבָר (ἄσχημον πρᾶγμα in the
Septuagint). Just what that indecency might involve is
left as undetermined in Matthew 5:32 as it is in
Deuteronomy 24:1; but the fact remains that the
Matthean form of the saying concerning divorce is
expressly not such as to abolish the Mosaic
prescription.

Within the Matthean presentation, therefore, the
precise relation of Jesus' teaching to Moses' command
is problematic. Jesus is held to affirm the very text
he might appear to supersede. The issue raised by the
"Pharisees" in 19:3 has particular moment within the
Matthean presentation: is it appropriate to divorce
"for any reason," or is the reference to the exceptive
clause from Deuteronomy in Jesus' teaching of 5:31, 32
merely formal? The question is almost a taunt, and it
implies some knowledge (at least on the reader's part)
of Jesus' position, and of potential contradictions
within it. Indeed, the passage is placed immediately
after Jesus' discourse to his disciples (18:1-19:1),
which concerns most directly the ordering of the
Matthean community. What is put in the mouths of
opponents is actually an issue within the Matthean
circles of Jesus' followers. The rhetorical
confrontation with opponents adds bite to the
question, but the question itself is more sensibly
seen as reflecting an intramural dispute, as in the
case of the Gentile leaders' mocking observation to
Yoḥanan ben Zakkai.

The "Pharisees" press the case in 19:7, by
asking exactly how Jesus' teaching squares with the
command of Moses. They ask what the community of

Matthew needs to know, and they do so with the added
vividness of the historic present. The response of
Jesus in v. 8 (again, in the historic present) grants
that Moses admitted of divorce, "for your hardness of
heart." The shift to the second-person, plural usage,
coming after the gnomic, third-person imperative in
respect of marriage in v. 6b, is notable. It is but a
whiff of the stronger statement later in Matthew, that
the Pharisees provide no model for behavior, despite
the validity of their halakhoth (23:2, 3). Matthew's
readers are expected to practice a greater
righteousness (5:20). The saying against divorce is
repeated, with a clause of exception, in 19:9, but the
grounds on which "indecency" might be established are
not spelled out.

The response of Jesus' disciples in 19:10
appears entirely appropriate: in the absence of stated
grounds of escape from marriage, its attractiveness is
reduced. That leads to the uniquely Matthean saying
about eunuchs, which is redolent of the sort of
hyperbole found in the extensions of the "Sermon on
the Mount." To read 19:10-12 outside the context of
the hyperbolic extensions, of course, is entirely
possible, and the youthful Origen did so in a manner
which precluded the possibility of his changing his
mind, except theoretically (see Eusebius, *The History
of the Church* 6.8.1, and A. H. McNeile [1957] 276).
The cumulative force of Matthew 19:3-12 is to urge
(although not to command) celibacy, albeit not by
means of a logical argument. Marriage is said to
establish an indivisible union according to God's
intention, and the divine institution of marriage is
held to undermine the propriety of discussing divorce
(vv. 3-6). The issue of Deuteronomy 24:1-4 therefore
becomes crucial, because its applicability appears
problematic. The solution is to restrict the
application of the Mosaic prescription, while
affirming its validity. Divorce is only provided in
view of "hardness of heart," and for "you," i.e., the
Pharisees (vv. 7, 8); other cases would amount to
adultery (v. 9). The implication is that non-Pharisaic
divorce is not regularized, which is the point of

departure for the disciples' down-hearted question and
the recommendation of celibacy (vv. 10-12). The scenic
movement from the debate with Pharisees to discussion
with the disciples (which is reminiscent of the
"Sermon on the Mount") is part of the rhetorical
stucture of the passage overall.

The Markan version of the dispute is cast in
different terms:

> And they were asking him if it were fitting for a
> man to divorce a wife, testing him. He answered
> them, What did Moses command you? They said,
> Moses permitted him to write a certificate of
> dissolution, and to divorce. Jesus said to them,
> For your hardness of heart he wrote you this
> commandment, but from the beginning of creation
> he made them male and female. On account of this
> a man shall leave his father and his mother, and
> the two will be one flesh. So they are no longer
> two, but one flesh. A man should not, then,
> divide what God has paired. And in the house the
> disciples again asked concerning this. He says to
> them, Whoever divorces his wife and marries
> another, commits adultery against her, and if she
> divorces her husband and marries another, she
> commits adultery.

Outside the "Western" text, the impersonal "they" of
the introduction is specified as "Pharisees," who
approach Jesus to test him (10:2). Because the
impersonal plural is a feature of Markan style, the
specification may be taken as an intrusive reading
from Matthew, the most widely used Gospel in the early
Church. Paul Ellingworth (1979) has argued that v. 10
favors the shorter reading. If the disciples ask him
"again," in another setting, they must have been the
subject envisaged in v. 2, where the same issue is
addressed. Ellingworth's approach is attractive, in
that he relates textual and contextual considerations,
but his solution itself poses exegetical difficulties.
In Mark, Jesus is elsewhere only "tested" by Satan
(1:13), Pharisees (8:11), and Pharisees with Herodians

(12:15), that is, by specified opponents. The
antagonism of the question in 10:2 is therefore
implicit in the setting, and is out of keeping with
the attitude of disciples (who are generally portrayed
as obtuse, rather than as deliberately obstructive).

A closer inspection of scenic context in chapter
10 helps to resolve the issue, and lends qualified
support to Ellingworth's position. A "crowd" is said
to gather around Jesus in Judaea, and he is described
as teaching them in the usual way (ὡς εἰώθει, 10:1).
The impersonal "they" of 10:2 would therefore refer to
an unsympathetic group within the crowd, which also
included disciples (10:10). Within chapter 10, a
similar tension between disciples and a larger
audience is exploited. "They" bring children to Jesus,
and earn the rebuke of disciples, but the approval of
their master (10:13-16). In sum, a pattern of
presentation is evident, in which the stance of those
in the crowd is contrasted (both negatively and
positively) with the stance of the disciples. The
notice that the question in 10:2 was a matter of
"testing" Jesus would suggest that a group of
opponents was within the crowd. Their specification as
Pharisees might well have come naturally to any
copyist who was familiar with the Matthean version of
the debate, in which the Pharisaic identity of the
opponents is rhetorically significant (as we have
observed).

Within the Markan scheme of presentation, the
rhetoric develops in a different fashion. The "crowds"
of 10:2 are in a similar position to the crowd in 4:1,
to whom the parable of the sower is told (4:3-9). The
earlier crowd includes "those outside," who do not
understand (4:11, 12); the disciples ask (4:10) and
receive (vv. 13-20) additional explanation. In chapter
10, as well, a mark of discipleship is to inquire
further of Jesus, and to hear his explanation
(10:10-12). A mark of the questioners' antipathy is
not only that they are said to "test" Jesus (10:2),
but that they are met by a counter-question (10:3, see
11:29). As a result, it is they who raise the issue of
Deuteronomy 24:1-4 (10:4), to which Jesus replies by

citing Genesis 1:27; 2:24. The order of presentation is reversed, as compared to Matthew, and the resolution of the passages from Genesis and Deuteronomy, by means of an exceptive clause, is not achieved. By the end of v. 9, the question of fitting divorce is itself rejected as unsuitable, but the place of Deuteronomy 24:1-4 is left unexplained.

Even Mark's Jesus, however, admits that Deuteronomy 24:1-4 is a command written as part of scripture (10:5). It is sometimes argued that the force of Jesus' argument in Mark is "to obliterate the Mosaic tolerance" (see W.L. Lane [1974] 355). But Jesus simply insists that divorce is provided in view of "hardness of heart," not by divine intention. Divorce is seen as an extraordinary provision, given to account for human weakness, not as prescriptive in any sense. The only way to evade that understanding is to assert that Jesus deliberately went about overturning the authority of scripture. But even in Mark 7, where Jesus is said radically to question received tradition, he complains that his interlocutors abrogate the word of God given to Moses (7:9-13); the "commandment of God" (7:8, 9) must in his view be honored, not broken. Mark's Jesus acknowledges that Deuteronomy 24:1-4 amounts to such a commandment in 10:3, 5, so that it seems strange to insist that Mark presents Jesus as invalidating Mosaic teaching in the case of divorce.

What of those who avail themselves of this barely permissible tolerance? That is the issue raised and addressed in 10:10-12. The language of adultery is hyperbolic, as in Matthew. We are prepared for hyperbole by the recommendation of suicide and self-mutilation, in order to avoid offending "one of these little ones," which precedes (9:42-50). And the legal reality of "committing adultery against her" is spurious, since adultery was a matter of taking another man's wife (see K. Berger [1972] 530-533, 536, 537). Yet 10:11 imagines the crime against the first wife, and v. 12 imagines a woman initiating the proceedings of divorce, which was not in her power. (The Graeco-Roman setting of the saying is commonly argued on that basis, but even within the Mishnah, women could compel divorce, although proceedings could not be initiated by them; cf. Nedarim 11:12; Kethuboth 5:5; 7:2-5, 9-10.) Within the argument of the entire pericope, where Deuteronomy 24:1-4 is not contradicted, divorce is obviously and hyperbolically condemned, but not excluded absolutely.

As compared to the subtle argument which has preceded, Luke 16:18 appears nothing if not succinct:

> Everyone who divorces his wife and marries another commits adultery, and he who marries someone divorced from a husband commits adultery.

The statement in Luke is the most vigorously worded attack on the practice of divorce in the New Testament. The active verb μοικεύω is used to characterize divorce and marriage with a divorcée, and its sense is plainer than is μοικάομαι in Matthew and Mark. There is no contextual mention of Deuteronomy 24, as in Matthew 19 and Mark 10; unlike Matthew 5:32, where there is also little by way of literary context, there is no exceptive clause to protect the place of Deuteronomy 24. Superficially, therefore, the saying can be construed as a blanket condemnation of divorce in any form.

The placement of the saying, however, seems to allude to a wider discussion than is actually presented in Luke. In v. 16, the assertion is made, "The law and the prophets were until John," from that point onward, the kingdom of God is preached, and becomes available (see Chilton [1979] 203-230). Such a strong emphasis on the kingdom's availability raises the implicit question: what of the law and the prophets now? That issue is addressed in v. 17, with the insistence that they continue to be of value: "It is easier for heaven and earth to disappear than for one serif of the law to drop." The saying about divorce then follows. Unless the reader has some understanding that Luke 16:18 does not contradict the Mosaic prescription, it must seem a non sequitur. But given such an understanding, the saying is in fact an illustration of how the kingdom involves a fresh stringency, not an abrogation, of the law. Precisely that illustrative force is what the placement of this abbreviated assertion presupposes.

SYNOPSIS SYNOPTICORUM

In general terms, the story of Yoḥanan and the disappearing Levites has prepared us for the relation among the stories in Matthew, Mark, and Luke. Mark, like Bekharoth in the Babli, presents us with the most common form of the haggadah; Luke, like Sanhedrin in the Yerushalmi, provides a version so garbled in its abbreviation as to be liable to misunderstanding; Matthew, like Numbers Rabbah, offers an intercalation of related material which substantially influences one's view of the teaching concerned. Moreover, each of the three Gospels, like their rabbinic analogues (*mutatis mutandis*), refers distinctively to the interlocutory context in which the teaching of Jesus is enunciated, and so shapes the way in which the reader might apply it. The alteration in interior structure between Matthew and Mark, however, is a fresh departure, as compared to what we have observed in the case of the teaching of Yoḥanan, and the Gospels' variations on the whole may appear more dramatic than what we have so far been prepared to expect from the Talmuds and Midrash Rabbah.

Before we can proceed to discuss the relative synopticity of the two sets of passages, however, it is necessary to develop some means of doing so, as the discussion to date has been conducted only in a notional way. Indeed, the preceding paragraph is a representative example of attempts to characterize degrees of synoptic deviation: the argument is made here that such deviation is greater in the case of the Gospels than in that of the rabbinic analogues, but the observation depends entirely upon exegetical considerations, subjectively weighed. Generally speaking, scholars of the Synoptic Gospels have argued that the relationship among their documents is closer than that manifest in rabbinic literature, so that

some reserve in respect of our initial finding may be
appropriate. In the nature of the case, exegesis must
be the foundational discipline in any comparison of
texts, but some means of analytic comparison may also
appear desirable. That need has in the past seemed to
have been met by Griesbach's invention of the
synopsis, a graphic arrangement of identity and
variation among texts.

The printing of comparable material in the form
of a synoptic table (of whatever format), however,
might itself tend to prejudice consideration. By
arranging lines of pericopae according to the
similarity of their content and wording, visual
conflation is achieved, and the inference is naturally
drawn (by any alert, and especially by the semi-alert,
reader) that a visually comparative exercise produced
the raw material so compared. A synoptic format may
therefore conceal precisely those phenomena which are
most troublesome: wordings which are not easily
understood as visual derivations may appear to be so,
just because they are aligned in parallel columns.

In order to avoid the constraints of a
tendentious, graphic presentation, an arithmetic
standard of comparison might be preferable.
Inevitably, such a standard will appear an arbitrary
means of analysis, but since its value is only
heuristic, consistent application to all the forms of
synopticity which are to be assessed should provide a
useful criterion of investigation. It should be
stressed that any such formula would not "solve" a
problem of synoptic relation, nor would it even
determine the medium (scribal, oral, or coincidental)
in which the comparability of texts emerged. But it
would serve as a benchmark against which other
instances of synopticity might be judged.

In evolving a formula of analysis, categories of
comparability have been accommodated, which ought to
be features of any synoptic comparison of texts.
Because a relatively simple formula is desirable, only
computations of words and their crude relations are
admissible. So far as is possible, judgments of
quality (e.g., content, and the meanings of words)

should not be entertained, since they are not susceptible of arithmetic measurement. First, the total number of words in a given passage is a relevant consideration. Of those, the number of identical words, and the number of identical words in the same syntax, are crucial considerations. If length, diction, and syntax are equal, two stories would be judged equivalent. Obviously, even in such an apparently straightforward case, an arithmetic judgment would need to be overturned, if the structure of two passages were globally different, or if the sense of their words differed significantly. Aside from such evidently important exegetical considerations, a difficulty emerges at the purely arithmetic level when documents diverge from one another: how should the factors of length, diction and syntax be weighted for the purposes of comparison?

In the absence of any certain, theoretical guide, and in the interests of simplicity, we propose an equal weighting of those factors which are computable in a scheme designed to generate a percentage. The formula is designed to measure the comparability of two passages, "a" and "b," according to their length ("l"), identity of diction ("d"), and syntactical congruence in cases of dictional identity ("s").

In each case, the length of the longer document is used to divide that of the shorter, yielding the value of "l." "d" is computed in two ways, each of which is weighted equally. "d (a)" is the dividend produced by dividing the number of words which are identical in "a" and "b" by the number of words in "a" overall; "d (b)" is the dividend produced by dividing the number of words which are identical in "a" and "b" by the number of words in "b" overall. "s" is also a proportion; the number of identical words which appear in the same syntax is divided by the number of identical words globally. "l," "d (a)," "d(b)," and "s" are all expressed by means of percentage (rounded), and averaged equally in order to provide an arithmetic rate of synopticity.

If we compare the passages in Bekharoth and
Sanhedrin, we arrive at the following raw data:

Bekharoth employs 37 words, of which 13 tally
exactly with Sanhedrin (4 being very similar),
and 12 words are used in the same syntax.

Sanhedrin, in its comparable unit, uses 25 words,
of which 13, 4, and 12 are the relevant factors
prevailing.

A proportional comparison of Bekharoth and Sanhedrin
is therefore straightforward, and by following the
formula proposed, the variables emerge as follows:

l=68%
d (Bekharoth)=46%
d (Sanhedrin)=68%
s=71%.

The global result, averaging the above figures, is
63%. It must be acknowledged, however, that in "d"
above (for both documents), similar words are counted
with identical words (see Appendix I). "d (Bekharoth)"
is reduced to 35%, and "d (Sanhedrin)" to 52%, if the
values are computed according to strict verbal
identify; on the other hand, "s" rises to 92%. The
revised values yield a resultantly global rate of 62%,
so that the final figure of synopticity might be taken
as 62%.
     The last figure attained can now be used to
assess the comparability of Bekharoth and Numbers
Rabbah (cf. Appendix I), where the values are:

l=17%
d (Bekharoth)=84%
d (Numbers Rabbah)=14%
s=68%.

The resultant average is 46%. "d Bekharoth" is reduced
to 81%, and "d (Numbers Rabbah) stays at 14%, when
strict identity is computed, and "s" rises to 70%,

which yields an average of just under 46%, a rate
which remains the index of comparability in this case.

So far, then, the rates of synopticity are 62%
for Bekharoth and Sanhedrin, and 46% for Bekharoth and
Numbers Rabbah. Sanhedrin and Bekharoth are related by
the same 62% that has already been computed, and
Sanhedrin and Numbers Rabbah by 33%. (Cf. Appendix I;
from this point onward, computations will be explained
less fully.) Numbers Rabbah is related to Bekharoth
and Sanhedrin respectively by the 46% and the 33%
which have already been computed. The totality of
computed relations averages at 47%, the rate of
synopticity which these texts manifest in aggregate.
Bekharoth agrees with its partners at a rate of 54%,
Sanhedrin with its partners at a rate of 48%, and
Numbers Rabbah with its partners at a rate of 40%.

Comparison with the analogous computations of
the passages in the Gospels is instructive. Matthew
relates to Mark at a rate of 67%: "l"is 68%, "d
(Matthew)" 51%, "d (Mark)" 75% and "s" 74% (cf.
Appendix I). That rate declines dramatically for
Matthew's relation to Luke, which comes out at 28%
(with values of 9%, 7%, 71% and 23% respectively).
Mark relates to Matthew at the 67% just mentioned, and
to Luke at 33% at most (13%, 12%, 88%, 27%). Luke
relates to Matthew at 28%, and to Mark at 35%. The
average rate of synopticity if therefore 43%, just 4
points below the rate of the rabbinic documents cited
above. Mark agrees with its partners at a rate of 51%
(as compared to 54% in the case of Bekharoth), Luke
agrees with its partners at a rate of 31% (cf.
Sanhedrin, at 48%), and Matthew with its partners at a
rate of 48% (cf. Numbers Rabbah, at 40%).

Certain observations regarding these data may
now be in order. Within the relations of each set of
documents, it is notable that the briefest pericope
(Sanhedrin or Luke) does not have the greatest rate of
correspondence. In both cases, that fact is not merely
a function of a consideration of length, but is also
explicable by the close relationship of the two longer
passages (Berkharoth and Numbers Rabbah; Matthew and
Mark). On the other hand, in both cases, the pericope

of median length (Bekharoth and Mark) is the most
representative, as might be expected under a
substantively synoptic relationship. As we compare the
rates of synopticity between the two sets of
documents, the lower rate of the Gospels is striking.

The difference appears to be a function of the
distinctive tendencies by which the respective sets of
pericopae were framed. Sanhedrin is substantively,
however garbled it may appear at first sight, an
abbreviation of the sort of story we can read in
fuller form in Bekharoth and Numbers Rabbah. But Luke
16:18 is not simply an abbreviation of Jesus' dispute
concerning divorce: it is the merest fragment thereof.
The change of synoptic rate, from 48% for Sanhedrin to
31% for Luke, is therefore no accident, but the
numerical index of what any reader might see. Once the
actual content of the passages is taken into account,
it is plain also that the 46% rate of synopticity for
Bekharoth and Numbers Rabbah attests a much closer
relationship than does the 67% of Matthew and Mark.
The additional material in Numbers Rabbah is either
logical explanation, or fuller description of the
exegetical issue that underlies Bekharoth; in Matthew,
the expansion represents a change in subject.
Moreover, numerical computation, as represented by the
formula suggested, does nothing whatever to reflect
the inversion in order between Matthew and Mark.
Indeed, the inversion is concealed by the numbers, in
that words used in distinctive contexts are treated as
identical in view of their morphology, no matter what
their meaning.

We might generalize the position, by saying that
the rabbinic texts manifest considerable variation,
and that the Synoptic Gospels manifest considerably
more. That generalization is all the more striking,
when we recall that the rabbinic documents concerned
took shape over a much longer period than Matthew,
Mark, and Luke did. Yerushalmi and Babli might be
placed within a century of one another (400-500), but
Numbers Rabbah amounts to an addendum within Midrash
Rabbah, and may be dated within the twelfth century.
The underlying typology of the haggadah nonetheless is

constant among the documents: a Gentile asks a mocking
question of Yoḥanan in an attempt to impugn Moses, and
is rebuffed. No alteration or addition changes that
typology, or the subject. Both are changed as one
moves among Matthew, Mark, and Luke. The statement
about divorce may be directed to enemies (Matthew), a
crowd (Mark), or disciples (Luke); it may or may not
focus on Moses, and may or may not recommend a form of
castration in view of the kingdom.

Our recourse to a heuristic, arithmetic formula
in order to assess synopticity has provided an index
of what may be confirmed by a comparative exegesis. It
might be considered sufficiently useful to justify the
application of such a formula to a larger sampling of
data. Whether or not it is as interesting a tool as
that, the fact remains that the arithmetic instrument
no more than suggested what only exegesis could
confirm, and much of the statistical data itself
required interpretation, in order to be analyzed
sensibly. The state of affairs certainly does not
refute the propriety of using such a formula, but
neither does it vindicate the procedure. Rather, the
entire exercise achieves no more than an insistence
that our procedure must be exegetical, or nothing at
all. But the exegetical finding, supported
arithmetically, is evident: *the well worn observation,
that Rabbinica manifest more variation than the
Synoptics, is -- at the level of the pericopae
presented -- simply false.* The fact of the matter in
the present case is that the transmission of materials
is more conservative within the sources of Judaism.

BATH QOL: THE CASES OF HILLEL AND JESUS

Among Jesus' contemporaries, the most renowned in the rabbinic literature which has survived is Hillel, a Babylonian sage whose expertise in the oral tradition made him a central figure of the first century, even in Palestine. Indeed, the story of his emergence as a leader focuses on his teaching, developed from Shemaiah and Abtalion, that Passover is of such importance as to override prescriptions concerning the sabbath. Neusner ([1985] 97-123) has presented that story synoptically, together with some of the more interesting material from the point of view of Hillel's halakhic authority, especially as contrasted with that of Shammai. (In the last study, Hillel's distinctive, but representative, position in respect of divorce was instanced.) Hillel was also the principal in a famous story in which he accepted a proselyte more readily than Shammai, and taught, "That which you hate, do not do to your fellow. That is the entire Torah, while all the rest is commentary thereon. Go and learn it" (cf. Shabbath 31a). Such materials have aroused considerable interest during this century in comparison with the position attributed to Jesus. Quite evidently, however, we need comparatively to assess the sources which refer to such figures, before any comparison of them as historical persons can be undertaken. Indeed, the same must be said of the comparison of Jesus with any such rabbi, for example Ḥanina ben Dosa, who is glibly adduced as a model for Jesus' ministry by G. Vermes ([1973] 72-80), without any critical argument whatsoever.

Hillel was held in such high esteem that he was thought worthy to receive the holy spirit. That estimate appears all the more exalted, but also strangely wistful, when it is borne in mind that the rabbis held that the spirit had been withdrawn since the time of the last prophets of scripture (cf. Schäfer [1972]). These motifs are drawn together in a most exciting manner in Tosefta Sotah 13:3 (cf. Neusner [1985] 114, 115):

Until the dead live, namely Haggai, Zechariah,
and Malachi, the latter prophets, the holy spirit
has ceased from Israel. Yet even so, they made
them hear bath qol. An example: the sages
gathered at the house of Guria in Jericho, and
they heard a bath qol saying, There is here a man
who is predestined for the holy spirit, except
that his generation is not righteous for such.
And they put their eyes on Hillel the elder, and
when he died, they said of him, Woe the meek man,
Woe, the faithful disciple of Ezra.

On first acquaintance, this haggadah is simply -- and
evocatively -- poignant of rabbinic virtue. There is
an apparent naïveté in the way the passage begins with
a general statement, concerning the general efficacy
of the angelic echo (bath qol), and is taken over by
the particular vignette concerning Hillel. In fact,
however, the rhetoric of the haggadah presses home its
central theme, that the prophetic authority of a
Haggai, a Zechariah, or a Malachi, is now to be
understood as reflected -- if only dimly -- in the
succession to Hillel the elder.

Hillel is not overtly designated as worthy of
the holy spirit by the angelic echo alone, but is so
identified jointly by the deflected voice of the
heavenly court and the sages gathered in Jericho. The
two operate together, because authority is now a
matter of consensus, not merely of charismatic
confirmation. (Such an orientation was established by
the famous story which pitted the great Eliezer ben
Hyrkanus against the majority, in the incident of the
stove of Akhnai [Babba Metzia 59a, b]. Despite
Eliezer's reversal of the flow of a stream, his
successful command that the walls of a schoolhouse
shake, and his designation as correct in his teaching
by a bath qol, the majority overturned his judgment of
the stove's uncleanness. And the Holy One, blessed be
he, laughed his pleasure, as Elijah himself later told
one of the rabbis.) The consensus concerned, however,
was not merely the rule of a contemporaneous majority,
but the cherished articulation of oral Torah
promulgated from the time of, and in succession to,

Ezra (cf. Avoth 1:1). That is why the final words of the vignette concerning Hillel ("Woe, the faithful disciple of Ezra") are tellingly apposite. The version of the haggadah in Babli (Sanhedrin 11a and Sotah 48b) is substantially similar to the Toseftan passage (cf. Appendix II), except that Hillel is said to be predestined "that the Shekhinah should dwell upon him as Moses our rabbi." The change does not mark a shift in direction, but it does betray an alteration in the ideological framework within which the authority of Hillel is understood to operate. As Neusner remarks ([1985] 116), "Shekhinah" might be taken as an idiomatic replacement of "the holy spirit" in Tosefta, but the fields of meaning within which the two terms operate are distinctive. Both may be said to involve prophecy and Temple, but the spirit principally concerns the former, and Shekhinah primarily the latter (cf. Chilton [1982] 48-52, 69-75). A concern with the succession to a cultically accessible Shekhinah is precisely the issue, then, which Babli characteristically addresses. Similarly, for Babli the fundamental lineament of authority is to be derived, not from Ezra, but from Moses. Accordingly, the comparison with Hillel is of Mosaic proportions, although Moses had to do with the Temple (and therefore with the Shekhinah, as a presence within the standard cult) only in the proleptic concerns of the written Torah, and in the living prescriptions of Mishnah, the oral Torah. In that both derived ultimately from Moses, the comparison in Babli has an interior logic as compelling as that of Tosefta.

Given the well articulated, distinctive, but also coordinated arguments of Tosefta and the two passages in Babli, an alternative development contained in Yerushalmi is notable. In Yerushalmi (Sotah 9:13), two other examples of the efficacy of bath qol are offered, before the story of Hillel is told:

Example: Simeon the righteous heard a bath qol going forth from the holy of holies, and it said, Gysgulyqas has been slain, and his decrees are void. Example: When young men went forth to make

war with Antychia, and Yoḥanan the high priest
heard a bath qol going forth from the holy of
holies, and saying, The young men who waged war
with Antychia have prevailed. And they wrote down
its time, and gave the moment, and they
established it had come at that hour.

The third example is that of Hillel, given much as in
Tosefta and Babli, except that the name of the sage of
Jericho is given as Gadia, rather than as Guria. But
the preceding two instances each have lives of their
own in both Tosefta and Babli.
    The story of Simeon is given separately from
that of Hillel in Tosefta Sotah 13:7 and Sotah 33a
(cf. Neusner [1985] 40, 41); as Neusner observes,
there seems little future in identifying "Gysgulyqas"
(or its its variant spellings) with Gaius Caligula, or
with any specified ruler. The contextual point is
rather either (as in Yerushalmi) that there is an
identifiable continuity of sages who enjoyed the
information of bath qol, or (as in Tosefta and Sotah)
that the bath qol brought a particular message, in its
own language (Aramaic, as the latter two versions have
it). Each haggadah carries just the material freight
apposite for its rhetorical function. The substantive
co-ordination of the material and the rhetorical
aspects of the haggadoth, however, is more evident
than explicable; which of the versions (if any) is the
most primitive remains a matter for speculation.
Similarly, the story of Yoḥanan is repeated in Tosefta
(Sotah 13:5) and Babli (Sotah 33a), but within the
program of discussing the nature of the bath qol and
not in the location assigned it in Yerushalmi (cf.
Neusner [1985] 90). Form and function are wedded so
perfectly as to make the distinction between the two
problematic.
    From the point of view of the present inquiry,
the phenomenon which is most striking is the finitude
of the elements related synoptically in Tosefta, Babli
and Yerushalmi. The apparently intrusive matter in
Yerushalmi is, it transpires, also present in the
other two documents, albeit in different positions,
and for distinctive purposes. And even the dislocating

presence of the material in Yerushalmi is not without its logic, as one reads the story of Hillel in Babli: is it not stated there, in both Sanhedrin and Sotah, that the *Shekhinah* is Hillel's inheritance? Consciously or not, the development of an association with the Temple is therefore well within the theological horizon which is envisaged, so that the association in Yerushalmi of Hillel's both qol with Simeon's (heard from the holy of holies) and with Yoḥanan's (as high priest) is quite explicable.

Closely related, but variegated portrayals of the address of a bath qol are also presented in the Synoptic Gospels, in the passage commonly referred to as the "transfiguration." In the Markan version, which is the most representative of the Synoptics generally, Jesus takes Peter, James, and John up a mountain six days after a discourse (9:2), where his garments shine white (v. 3). Elijah and Moses appear (v. 4), and a discomfited Peter offers to build booths (vv. 5, 6). A cloud then overshadows the disciples, and a voice proceeds from it, "This is my beloved son, hear him" (v. 7).

In an article which appeared some years ago, I detailed the provenience of the major elements in the passage, as deriving from Exodus 24 (cf. Chilton [1980] 120-123). At the close of the story in Exodus, Moses is said to ascend the mountain, when a cloud, closely associated with God's glory, covered it (v. 15). The covering lasted six days, after which time, the LORD called to Moses (v. 16), who entered the fiery realm of glory forty days and forty nights (vv. 17, 18). Earlier in the chapter, Moses is commanded to take three worshipers, Aaron, Nadab, and Abihu, together with seventy elders, in order to confirm the covenant (vv. 1-8). The result is that just these people (v. 9) are explicitly said to have seen "the God of Israel" in his court (v. 10) and to celebrate their vision (v. 11). (The statement, of course, raises theological questions, as the Targumic versions of the passages indicate; they will be discussed in Study 4.) The motifs of master, three disciples, mountain, cloud, vision and audition, are held in common between Exodus 24 and Mark 9.

There is no sense in which it is fruitful, or
even possible, to describe the transfiguration as a
"midrash" of Exodus 24. The interests of commentary
upon an earlier scripture, however loosely one might
define those interests as evidenced in the various
sorts of midrashim (cf. Chilton [1983] and Neusner
[1987]), are simply not served by the Markan text.
Indeed, even if one were to widen the circle of the
genre, to include works in which Scripture is
rewritten, as in the Genesis Apocryphon (cf. Bauckham
[1983]), no useful analogy with the transfiguration is
discovered, since those elements in Exodus 24 which
have some echo in Mark 9 are scrambled, in their order
of appearance and setting, and several crucial
elements (cf. the action in Exodus 24:12-14, as
compared to vv. 1, 2) find no answering echo in Mark.

As is perhaps even more fatal to any analysis of
the transfiguration which relies upon the category of
"midrash," the structurally central climax of Mark 9
differs from that of Exodus 24. In fact, Exodus 24 is
itself but a preamble to the divine instructions which
commence properly in chapter 25. What happens on the
mountain designates Moses, in narrative and visionary
terms, as the single spokesman of revelation (cf. v.
18, in particular); others in the chapter are present,
only to be excluded at the pivotal moment of divine
disclosure. They join in the celebration of divine
vision (vv. 9-11), but they do not hear what Moses
hears. By contrast, the climax of the transfiguration,
the apogee of tension and the interpretative key, is
precisely 9:7, when the voice addresses, not Jesus
alone, but the three. The bath qol is no accoutrement
of the narrative, but the very focus of interest.

The last point emerges all the more clearly when
Mark 9 is compared with the story concerning Hillel in
Tosefta. Evidently, each is a haggadah whose force is
recognized when the bath qol speaks. The
transfiguration emerges quite evidently as such a
haggadah, rather than a displaced portrait of Jesus'
resurrection, parousia, heavenly enthronement, or
ascension, as modern criticism would have it (cf.
Chilton [1980] 115, 116, 120-123). Indeed, the history
of discussion concerning this pericope in particular

demonstrates just how egregious an ignorance of
Judaica among scholars of the New Testament can be: in
the absence of categories developed from literature of
the period, stories are fitted into the most cherished
pigeon-holes of modern scholarship itself. The
practice of criticism in an intellectual ghetto of
Gentile (usually Protestant) ideology, in which the
New Testament is protected from Judaica with a wall of
self-referential, and repetitious, secondary
literature, remains the most fundamental flaw in the
discipline today. In the instance of the
transfiguration, it has resulted in the failure to
appreciate the force of the bath qol within the story,
a force which is all the more evident by comparison
with the Toseftan story concerning Hillel. For Mark's
account, unlike Tosefta's, has the bath qol interpret
its own significance, rather than utter words which
require explication by sages.

The shape of the Markan account harnesses the
energy of the self-explanatory bath qol in order to
drive a christological engine. The divine voice here
essentially repeats what is said in the baptismal
scene (1:11), but now in the hearing of the select
three disciples. For the first time in Mark, Jesus'
identity as God's son, known by the reader from the
outset (1:1), is promulgated in a manner the disciples
are intended to grasp. The placement of the story
after Jesus' identification as the son of man, who
must suffer (8:31), makes the transfiguration into the
baptism of Jesus' passion, much as the baptismal scene
itself initiates his ministry of preaching.

Obviously, the narrative embedding of the story
within Mark shifts the focus from the auditory and
visionary elements within the scene, to their
significance within the explicitly christological
interest of the Gospel's outline. Indeed, the
alteration appears to have caused a crucial
re-arrangement within the story. Discussion has long
focused on the perplexing saying of Jesus (9:1) which
precedes the transfiguration. The saying itself is
reformulated in each of the Synoptics (as compared to
the other two), but its position, prior to the
transfiguration, is stable among them. In the saying's

present position, when Jesus says that there are some standing in his presence who will not taste death until the kingdom (or, as in Matthew, the son of man) comes, the sense of the logion is that some of his disciples will survive until the eschaton.

Such a promise is consistent with the *Naherwartung* which is characteristic of Synoptic eschatology. But there are indications that an earlier placement of the logion was within the transfiguration, rather than as a preface to it (cf. Chilton [1979] 251-274 and Chilton [1980]). The first trace of the earlier placement within Mark is the usage of the adverb "here" (ὧδε) in the phrase, "there are here some of those standing." As was observed in the Introduction, the Matthean (16:28) parallel (as well as the Lukan [9:27], if the position of αὐτοῦ is read as analogous) demonstrates that the placement of Mark (εἰσίν τινες ὧδε τῶν ἑστηκότων, rather than εἰσίν τινες τῶν ὧδε...) is clumsy. The question emerges, to what does the odd placement draw attention? As it happens, Peter in the scene of the transfiguration, which follows, suggests rather lamely that it is good for the three disciples to be "here" (ὧδε, v. 5). "Here," understood as the locus of revelation, is also what 9:1 may originally have referred to. "Some standing here, who will never taste death" would then have referred, not to Jesus' disciples, but to those with Jesus in his transfiguration, Elijah and Moses, who are understood in Judaic tradition not to have tasted death.

Elijah's immortality is already attested in 2 Kings 2:9-12, and is well established within early and rabbinic Judaism (cf. Chilton [1979] 268-270). The statement in Deuteronomy 34:7, that Moses in fact died, did not prevent Josephus from describing Moses as disappearing (ἀφανίζεται) in the course of conversation with Eleazar and Joshua (Ἰησοῦς, *Antiquities* 4.8.48 @ 326). In that Josephus speaks of Elijah and Enoch with the cognate adjective, ἀφανεῖς, and uses the verb ἀφανίζομαι itself of Elijah (9.2.2 @ 28), his understanding that Moses was immortal seems evident; the scriptural notice that Moses' grave was a mystery (Deuteronomy 34:6) therefore acquired a life of its own. (Notably, and no doubt coincidentally, Josephus gives us two of the three -- Moses and "Jesus" [that is, Ιησοῦς, for "Joshua"] -- who appear in the transfiguration.) What place, however, would people who actually do not taste death have in the saying of Jesus? The answer may be provided by Targum Pseudo-Jonathan, at Deuteronomy 32:1, where Moses swears by witnesses "who will not taste death:" the heavens and the earth. To understand the deathless figures in that way obviously requires that Mark 9:1 be taken as an oath, but that brings us to the final observation: appreciated within Semitic syntax, the statement in any case appears asseverative.

When God says to Abraham in Genesis 28:15 that he will not forsake him until he does all he promised him, that is not an undertaking to do what he must, and then depart. Statements of that sort are rather to be seen as emphatic confirmations of their apodoses, not as limitations to the circumstances of their protases (cf. Chilton [1979] 272 and Beyer [1968] 132f.). The sense of the logion is, therefore, that there are "here deathless witnesses, Moses and Elijah, who attest the coming of the kingdom." As in the case of Hillel, the story is designed to draw attention to what is "here"(כאן in Tosefta) as divinely warranted reality. In the transfiguration Moses' mountain in Exodus 24, and Elijah's in 1 Kings 19, are united in a fresh theophany. Philo had understood Moses to have been changed to the divine on Sinai (*Questiones et Solutiones ad Exodum* 2.29); now a new mountain designates a son, sealed by a bath qol.

Such departures from agreement with Mark as are significant in Matthew and Luke tend to support a reading, along the lines suggested above, of the transfiguration as an account of theophanic disclosure. Matthew 17:6, 7 is unique, and expresses the great fear of the disciples, and Jesus' assurance, in a manner comparable with the uniquely Matthean addendum to the pericope of Jesus' walking on the sea, in which the disciples first confess their master to be God's son (14:28-33). Notably, the precise form of words used to describe the reaction of the disciples to the transfiguration, ἐφοβήθησαν σφόδρα, is exactly repeated at 27:54, where the reaction of the centurion and those with him to Jesus' death, and the subsequent earthquake, is described. Luke's version puts the events at eight, rather than six days' remove from the preceding discourse (9:28) and that distinction has long perplexed commentators. Within the context here proposed for understanding the transfiguration, that change is not predictable, but at least it may be explained. In Exodus 24:11, Nadab and Abihu are said in the Targum Pseudo-Jonathan to have been struck down as a result of their vision. That they should have been punished is straightforward, since Exodus 33:20 itself insists that what happens in 24:10 (a direct vision of God, which is limited to Nadab and Abihu in Pseudo-Jonathan) must not happen on pain of death. The motif of punishment, therefore, is derived logically from scripture, but the Targumic understanding in 24:11, that they were struck *eight* days after the vision, is an intersection with Luke 9:28 which it is difficult to attribute to pure coincidence. Certainly, such an argument becomes all but impossible to sustain, when Jesus is said to discuss his "exodus" (ἔξοδος with Moses and Elijah, v. 31), and when the disciples wake themselves from theophanic sleep to behold "glory" (v. 32, cf. 22:46 with Matthew 26:40-46 and Mark 14:37-42). Matthew (17:2) and Luke (9:29) together understand that Jesus' face shone, as did that of Moses (Exodus 34:29, 30). All three Synoptic Gospels refer to Jesus' white garments (Matthew 17:2; Mark 9:3; Luke 9:29); it is remarkable that (once again) divine garments are at issue in Pseudo-Jonathan Exodus 33:23, where in the Masoretic Text Moses sees the back of God.

Although the transfiguration can only be seen, within its setting in early Judaism, as a story concerning a bath qol, its complication within that genre is striking. Elements of theophanic language, involving the stories concerning Moses and Elijah, are woven into the narratives, such that the deviations of one narrative from the others is explicable within the terms of reference of that language. In that sense, the intrusively fresh element of two stories of a bath qol in connection with the Temple, in Yerushalmi's version of the pericope concerning Hillel, is substantively (and structurally) a greater departure than any variation within a Synoptic Gospel relative to its partners. (Nonetheless, the structural innovation manifest in Yerushalmi is not, as we have seen, arbitrary, nor is the theme thereby expressed entirely idiosyncratic.) As in the case of the last Study, the material synopticity of the rabbinic texts concerned is comparable with what is evidenced in the first three Gospels, but in the present instance, the substantive nexus of the Gospels' synopticity is greater, despite their greater number of variants from complete identity.

When the Gospel according to John is taken into account, the picture changes radically. Unlike in the case of Jesus' teaching concerning marriage, there is a Johannine analogy to the transfiguration in the Synoptics. In chapter twelve (vv. 27-33), the following vignette appears, commencing with direct discourse from Jesus:

> Now my soul is shaken, and what shall I say? Father, save me from this hour!? But for this very purpose I have come to his hour. Father, glorify your name! Then a voice came from heaven: I have glorified, and I shall glorify again! Then the crowd there, which heard, thought it had been thunder, but others said, An angel has spoken to him. Jesus replied, This voice has not come for me, but for you. Now is the judgment of this world, now shall the ruler of this world be utterly cast out. And if I am lifted up from the earth, I shall draw all people to myself. He said that to signify by what manner of death he was about to die.

The Johannine bath qol is linked to the motif of Jesus' death, as it is also (albeit by quite different means) in the Synoptic transfiguration. It is also notable that the saying which advises the abandonment of one's own soul appears before the narrative of the bath qol in all its incarnations (Matthew 16:25; Mark 8:35; Luke 9:24; John 12:25). That we are dealing with a Johannine analogue to the Synoptic transfiguration, in material and contextual terms, therefore appears obvious.

Equally obvious, however, is the substantial autonomy of the Johannine bath qol from the Synoptic bath qol. The Johannine voice has something different to say, and is heard by Jesus, its sole interpreter, while the crowd fails to understand. The account is embedded in typically Johannine themes, of the "hour" at which Jesus is to die, of his being "lifted up," and of the density of bystanders. To derive the Johannine bath qol from the Synoptic, or vice versa, appears impossible, unless one is committed on dogmatic grounds to the thesis that there must be a documentary connection. Structurally and substantially, the Johannine narrative is so different from its Synoptic counterpart, quite aside from its involvement with characteristically Johannine themes, that to speak of it as a version of the transfiguration is unwarranted. It is merely the nuanced story of a bath qol, more comparable to the story of Hillel than to the elaborately visionary development, by means of Exodus 24, which is evident in the transfiguration.

Indeed, the analogy *and* disanalogy of the Johannine bath qol with the transfiguration forces us to employ a language of comparison which does not presume genetic dependence. While Matthew, Mark, and Luke each offer a distinctive construal of essentially the same transfiguration, John offers, instead, a construal of another story, involving a certain understanding of Jesus and a bath qol. In both the Synoptic and the Johannine construals, a bath qol is involved, but the former texts transform the bath qol's significance into a visionary element, while the latter text transforms it into Jesus' discursive reference to his own death. What we have, that is to say, are not distinctive construals of a single story, but distinctive transformations of a comparable motif (Jesus and a bath qol, related both to discipleship and his own death). Just as it is problematic to speak of an order of precedence among the varying construals (whether of Jesus' transfiguration or Hillel's commendation), so the observation of related, but distinctive, transformations is not easily explained by simple precedence. In the present case, to suppose that John is dependent upon the transfiguration requires that we imagine a conscious aversion from a Mosaic motif, while a typology of Moses is evident in John (cf. Meeks [1967]). To reverse the equation of dependence is equally suspect, since that involves imagining that the tradents of the Synoptic transformation deliberately excised an overt reference to Jesus' death, which is one of the principal concerns of the first three Gospels at this point in all their narratives. Construals and transformations of tradition may be understood more readily by reference to one another, but to derive them genetically requires the ignorance, not the appreciation, of some of their most striking elements.

BIRDS AND PEOPLE -- THE GRASS IS ALWAYS GREENER...

An Aramaic idiom, "(the) son of (the) man" (a rendering to be explained) has recently received renewed attention, as providing a possible antecedent of the characteristically dominical expression, "the son of the man" (as a slavish translation of the Greek would have it). In Aramaic, the phrase essentially means "human being," and the issue which has emerged in the study of the Gospels centers on whether Jesus used the phrase with that broad, non-messianic reference. Amongst recent contributors, Geza Vermes has been the most conspicuous exponent of the view that the Aramaic idiom is the only key necessary for understanding Jesus' preaching, at least in this regard (cf. Vermes [1973] 160-191). His own particular generalization, that the phrase is a circumlocution for "I," has rightly been attacked (cf. Fitzymer [1979]): the fact is that "(the) son of (the) man" in Aramaic is generic, in the sense that, insofar as it is self-referential, the speaker is included in the class of human beings, but the class normally refers to mortal humanity, not to one human being alone (cf. Bowker [1977] and Chilton [1987] lvi-lvii).

One of the passages cited by Vermes, from Yerushalmi (Shebi'ith 9:1), should have made the last point entirely plain to him:

> Rabbi Simeon ben Yohai made a hide-out in a cave thirteen years, in a cave of carobs and dates, until his flesh came up scabby. At the end of thirteen years, he said, If I do not go forth to see (sic!) the voice of the world.... He went forth and sat at the mouth of the cave. He saw one hunter, hunting birds, spreading his net. He heard a bath qol saying, Release, and the bird was saved. He said, A bird apart from heaven will not perish, how much less (the) son of (the) man!

Quite evidently, the syllogism (such as it is) cannot function unless both "bird" and "(the) son of (the) man" are understood as classes of being, not particular entities. The point is that the divine care

for animals demonstrates by analogy that human beings
are not left hopeless, and Simeon goes on to leave the
cave. The genre of being which is described by "(the)
son of (the) man" obviously includes Simeon, since
otherwise, he could not reach the conclusion, and
undertake the action, which he does. But the genre is
no mere circumlocution for Simeon, since otherwise the
class could not be compared to that of which the bird
in the narrative is an instance, not the entire set.
(The generic quality of the phrase may be more
apparent if, as Aramaic grammar permits, the
determined state of "man" is not held to equate to the
usage of the definite article in English. As it
happens, בר נש ["son of man"] and בר נשא ["the son of
the man"] are virtually indistinguishable in usage.
That is the reason for the parenthetical qualification
of "the" here. It must also be pointed out that the
form in Jesus' time was probably בר אנש[א]; cf.
Fitzmyer [1979] 62.) If God cares for birds, and his
care for humans can be inferred therefrom, Simeon has
grounds for assurance; if his resolve to leave the
cave is based solely on his observation of a single
bird's illustration of his own destiny, his thinking
is wishful, not positively forceful.

The function of the bath qol is similar to what
we observed in Study 2: the heavenly voice requires
earthly explication. As in the case of the bath qol in
respect of Hillel, a new language is used, but in this
case Latin, "Release" (*dimissio*), rather than Aramaic.
Given the setting of the story, in the hard period
subsequent to the revolt of Bar Kokhba, when the Roman
Imperium exerted its power definitively over
Palestine, the language of the voice is apposite. A
version of the story with slightly more by way of
setting occurs in Genesis Rabbah 79:6; in that case,
Simeon also sees a bird taken when the voice cries
"*Spekula*". Even more clearly than in Yerushalmi, the
narrative concerns a genre of being, which is
comparable to the class of humanity, not to a
particular bird, in that Simeon decides that both he
and his son should leave the cave. Unfortunately,
Vermes does not observe this aspect of the story,
which is also found (substantively) in Ecclesiastes

Rabbah 10:8. All these versions are presented, neatly laid out, in Hugh Odeberg's *The Aramaic Portions of Bereshit Rabbah* ([1939] 92, 154-157), from which Vermes drew his examples ([1973] 257 n. 26).

The fact is also worth mentioning, since it has been consistently overlooked, that Odeberg called attention as well to the value of the story concerning Simeon for understanding the Gospels (p. 154). Vermes's claims of originality have been so exaggerated as to suggest that he for the first time identified the various versions of the haggadah, and for the first time related them to the Gospels (cf. Vermes [1978]). Neither claim is true. In addition to providing the fullest citation of the versions available (even today), Odeberg makes specific mention of Matthew 10:29, where Jesus insists that the very sparrows which are bought cheaply do not fall to earth apart from the father's will. By analogy, people ought to take comfort (v. 31). Odeberg observed that "apart from your father" in Matthew 10:29 is substantively equivalent to "apart from heaven" in Genesis Rabbah (and, one might add, Yerushalmi and Ecclesiastes Rabbah). His observation is confirmed, when one recalls that the phrase becomes "before God" in the Lukan equivalent of the saying (12:6, 7). (Luke 12:6 also envisions sparrows being "forgotten" [ἐπιλελησμένον], not falling, and they are cheaper than Matthew's birds; otherwise, the agreement with Matthew 10:29 is striking, albeit not verbatim.) It would appear that essentially the same observation of nature is employed by Jesus and Simeon. In the case of Jesus, the observation seems to urge carelessness upon disciples, in view of providence; in the case of Simeon, the lesson derived from the bird is courage in view of providence, and the observation is explicitly directed to Simeon himself (with his son, as relevant), although the transmission of the haggadah intimates that there is also a wider application.

Odeberg's comparison of the passages may be pressed further; it becomes evident that his laconic citation of a single verse from Matthew is an invitation to see the power of a theologoumenon as it unfolds in texts of differing periods and

circumstances. For just as the haggadah of Simeon is
directed to the circumstances of persecution, when the
Romans prowled for followers of a failed revolt, so
the haggadah of Jesus is couched in the form of advice
to those who confront the punishing power of civil
rulers (who "kill the body, but are not able to kill
the soul," Matthew 10:28, cf. Luke 12:4.) Underlying
the sayings of Jesus and Simeon, despite their evident
independence from a genetic point of view (be it at
the level of literary or of oral influence), is a
common, metaphorical transposition. The target of the
saying (disciples or Simeon) is compared to birds
which may perish (by natural causes or hunting), but
then the divine care for such humble creatures is used
to assure the target. In just this application of
assurance, Simeon's saying is aesthetically superior
to Jesus', because the image of the bird ensnared is
far more evocative (from the established perspectives
of both sayings) than that of the bird as fallen or
(worse still) forgotten.

A striking feature of a comparison of Jesus'
saying and Simeon's (again, passed over in silence by
Odeberg -- consciously or not -- in his laconic
citation), is that Jesus does *not* here employ the
theologoumenon "(the) son of (the) man" in any form.
That is, Jesus saying performs a meaning comparable to
Simeon's, by means of the same, essentially generic
contrast between birds and those people who are in
circumstances of persecution, but it does so without
reference to the phrase which concerns Vermes. In
itself, the question of the origins of the dominical
usage "the son of the man" cannot concern us here.
That is (still) a suitable subject for monographic
treatment. But it must at least be noted how
egregiously Vermes's failure to cite Odeberg fully has
distorted the course of recent research. Vermes has
been able to argue for an analogy between Jesus' and
rabbinic usage which is so perfect as to approach
identity, but only by ignoring evidence of obvious
disanalogy. Everyone who has ever read Odeberg knows
(1) that the usage is well and truly generic (not
circumlocutional, as Vermes would have it) and (2)
that Matthew 10:29-31 (with Luke 12:6, 7) represents a

tendency *not* to employ the usage when essentially the
same meaning as in Simeon's dictum is at issue. But
because Vermes failed adequately to cite Odeberg, in
his false pretension to originality, it has required
considerable discussion (and several contributions
from J. A. Fitzmyer) to establish the first point, and
scholars continue to be misled in respect of the
second. In his recent and otherwise excellent study of
"the son of the man" in the Gospels, Barnabas Lindars
(1983) cites Vermes's collection of haggadoth
concerning Simeon, and he also accepts the analogy
posited by Vermes with Jesus' usage. Had sound
scholarly technique stood behind Vermes's treatment,
Lindars would have been encouraged to include
Odeberg's analysis, in which it becomes evident that
"the son of the man" is not used generically in a
saying of Jesus (namely, Matthew 10:29-31; Luke 12:6,
7), when the comparison with the haggadah of the cave
might lead us to expect just that. In the event, both
Matthew (10:32, 33) and Luke (12:8, 9) have Jesus
refer to "the son of the man" immediately after his
remark concerning sparrows; in both cases, it
emphatically refers, not generically, but
particularly, to a specific figure in the heavenly
court. That fact is explicit within the Gospels. It
has been possible to ignore it within the most recent
discussion only because Dr Vermes ignored Prof.
Odeberg's insight.

As has already been suggested, no solution can
here be offered to the perplexing question of what the
dominical phrase, "the son of the man," refers to. Our
focus must rather be on another feature of the
comparison of haggadoth concerning Simeon and Jesus, a
feature which is a regular phenomenon of textual
comparison. In Study 1, we treated of texts in which a
single tradition (be it of Yoḥanan and the Levites or
of Jesus and the wives) occasioned construals of that
tradition which were mutually explicable. In Study 2,
we also discovered construals of the same essential
haggadah: the transfiguration, and the story of Hillel
and the bath qol. But in the case of Study 2, we also
encountered alternative developments within traditions
which went beyond what we might ordinarily refer to as

"construal." Within Yerushalmi, the additional instances of bath qol which are cited tend to shift the emphasis, from the exaltation of Hillel to the phenomenon of bath qol generally. Even more dramatically, the haggadah of Jesus and the bath qol in John 12 struck us as so distinctive a version of the tradition as to demand the designation of "transformation," rather than "construal." But now, as we compare the haggadoth concerning Jesus and Simeon, it is perfectly plain that we are dealing with neither construals nor transformations of a common tradition, for the simple reason that no common tradition evidently lies behind them.

The force of these observations is to the effect that Odeberg put his finger on an order of relationship between texts which does not demand the supposition of their genetic dependence upon the same tradition. "Simeon" and "Jesus" (or whichever speakers are represented by Yerushalmi, Genesis Rabbah, and Ecclesiastes Rabbah on the one hand, and by Matthew and Luke on the other hand) simply use a similar topos of the comparative value of the human and ornithological in order to provide assurance of divine care in the midst of real or potential persecution. Notably, their similarity in the conveyance of a cognate meaning by comparable means does not extend to the usage of the theologoumenon, "(the) son of (the) man." Simeon and Jesus are comparable -- and better understood in one another's light -- in respect of the meaning performed within haggadah attributed to them: they urge similar things by a single topos developed distinctively. But what they perform -- as far as presently can be seen -- are not the traditions of others (that would be construal or transformation), but their own insights within the theological language available to them. In other words, for all that their sayings are comparable, Simeon and Jesus have no need of a tertium quid, a yet more ancient dictum, to explicate for us why they say what they say. They simply speak, and traditions are created, which are then subject to haggadic construal and/or transformation. They are performers, not tradents. For the purposes of creating these sayings, they required only a language, eyes, ears, and a mouth; appeal to some prior tradition (in the absence of evidence to that effect) only distracts us from our enjoyment of the distinctive performances.

Indeed, it should be emphasized that our distinctions among performances, transformations, and construals are heuristic, in respect of readers' cognition: they appear sensible given the lay of texts at a given moment. A "performance" is not something actually said (or, for that matter, not said) by Simeon or Jesus at some time; it is a distinctive, autonomous conveyance of meaning within the language of early Judaism. A "transformation" is not a tradent's attempt to alter a performance, any more than a "construal" is a deliberate effort at nuance; they are simply the names we might use to describe greater or lesser degrees of congruence in that promulgation of performance which is known as tradition. "Simeon" and "Jesus" are, in the first instance, nothing more than names given to performances, just as "Yerushalmi," "Genesis Rabbah," "Ecclesiastes Rabbah," "Matthew," and "Luke" are, in the first instance, nothing other than names given to transformations and construals by anonymous tradents (orally and/or in writing) of such performances.

The relative absence of Simeon's theologoumenon, "(the) son of (the) man," from Jesus' saying should by itself alert us to the possibility, already mentioned, that it carries a different significance within Jesus' performance. Precisely that possibility comes evidently to expression in a saying in which "the son of the man" is employed, again in the material known as "Q" (Matthew 8:19, 20, cf. Luke 9:57, 58):

A scribe approached, and said to him, Teacher, I will follow you wherever you go. And Jesus says to him, The foxes have holes and the birds of heaven nests, but the son of the man has not a place where he might lay his head.

The saying explicitly addresses the issue of discipleship in both Gospels. The famous dictum, "Let the dead bury their own dead," follows in each case

(Matthew 8:21, 22; Luke 9:59, 60). Moreover, the same issue is developed within the construals of each Gospel.

In Matthew, a scribe is the interlocutor, and such figures in the first Gospel might be "trained for the kingdom" (13:52); that is evidently the understanding here, because the next interlocutor is described as "another of his disciples" (v. 21). The story of the stilling of the storm follows (vv. 23-27), a paradigmatic instance of discipleship.

The Lukan construal attains a cognate presentation of the saying, by its own means, as can be traced by observing the usage of the verb, "to travel" (πορεύεσθαι), within this complex of material. Jesus is said programmatically to "set his face to travel to Jerusalem" in 9:51, and he sends messengers before him (v. 52a). They proceed to "travel" (v. 52b), but do not manage to prepare a welcome for him in a village of Samaritans "because his face was traveling to Jerusalem" (v. 53). Jesus rebukes the manifestly odd suggestions that fire be called down from heaven (vv. 54, 55); rather, "they traveled to another village" (v. 56). It is, then, "While they were traveling on the way" that an unnamed interlocutor appears and says what is attributed to a scribe in Matthew (v. 57). But there is an addition to the Lukan complex. Just as Jesus' disciples had suggested they call down fire from heaven, in the manner of Elisha (cf. 2 Kings 1:10, 12), so the Lukan Jesus closes this group of sayings with the observation that no one who exercises domestic responsibility, by putting his hand to the plough in the manner of Elisha (1 Kings 19:20), is worthy of the kingdom (vv. 61, 62). The following material concerns the commissioning of seventy disciples, who promulgate precisely that kingdom (10:1-12, vv. 9, 11).

There is an evident adjustment of meaning involved as the reader moves from the Matthean to the Lukan construal of Jesus' saying in respect of foxes, birds, and the son of the man. What is in the former case a paradigm of scribal discipleship is in the latter case a paradigm of peripatetic discipleship. Nonetheless, Matthew and Luke share the understanding

that "the son of the man" is christologically
redolent, and that the issue of the saying is
discipleship in respect of precisely that "son of
man." Nothing intrinsic to the saying, within the
language of early Judaism, requires such a
presentation of it. "Son of man" need mean no more
than "person," and generally should not be pressed for
more meaning without warrant. Within that sense of the
phrase, it is hardly natural to understand the saying
in reference to discipleship. The exigencies of human
life are, perhaps, more plausibly at issue:

> Foxes have dens and birds their nests: only man
> has nowhere to lay his head.

If such a gnomic (if cynical) sense is held to have
been the performed meaning of the saying, then what we
see in Matthew and Luke is evidence of a fundamental
transformation of that meaning, into the new keys of
christology and discipleship.
     The question naturally arises, whether the
performed meaning posited in the last paragraph should
be ascribed to Jesus. At just this point, a note of
caution needs to be sounded. "The historical Jesus,"
who was bequeathed to us by the liberal theology of
the last century, was an empirically knowable figure,
who transcended the doctrines of Christianity. His
epitaph was written by two German scholars at the turn
of the century, Albert Schweitzer and William Wrede.
Schweitzer, for all his evident inadequacies (cf.
Chilton, *Kingdom* [1984] 8, 9, cf. Schweitzer [1954]),
did demonstrate that whatever Jesus said, thought, and
did, was -- historically speaking -- conditioned by
doctrinal constraints and religious perspectives no
less compelling than those which influence Christians
(and other religious people) generally. What has
chiefly alienated many readers of Schweitzer is his
perfectly sensible observation that the constraints
and perspectives in the case of Jesus were not
Christian in any definable sense, but Jewish and
eschatological. Rather more profoundly, Wrede (1901)
demonstrated that to search for data concerning Jesus
(as distinct from christological interpretations of

him) in the Gospels is as sensible as looking for
objectivity in a politically stirring speech. Attempts
to revive the sort of historical Jesus liberal
theology required, an archaeological datum which might
refute modern dogmatism, are fashionable only among
those who have remained unmoved by developments during
this century. Among Christians, certain conservatively
inclined Evangelicals, such as J. W. Wenham (1984) and
Michael Green (1984), continue to treat the Gospels as
if they were concocted as puzzles which contain all
the necessary facts of history, provided they are
re-arranged cleverly. Among certain Jewish
interpreters of Jesus, an equally astonishing naïveté
is apparent. Harvey Falk (1985) has recently
represented the attitude that the Gospels are to be
taken as relaying Jesus' ipsissima verba, and Vermes
apparently believes such data can be gleaned, provided
the texts are shorn of their hellenistic accretions
(cf. Vermes [1983] 85). Such manifest critical density
is simply not tolerable in scholarly discussion.

    Aside from "the historical Jesus" of liberal
Protestantism (and his ghost among badly informed
contributors), no other contenders have clearly
emerged as viable. "The new quest of the historical
Jesus" has been hailed from time to time in the period
since the war, but its claims have never been
realized. It was an attempt to discover the dialectic
between Bultmann's "Christ of faith," who required a
decision for or against himself in the texts as they
stand, and Bultmann's messianic prophet, the Judaic
teacher who could be investigated by historical means
(cf. Bultmann [1934]). In order to be successful, "the
new quest" required grounding in the sources of
Judaism, but its practitioners were even less skilled
in that regard than Bultmann himself was. Instead,
"new questers" of the 'fifties and 'sixties have
turned to "the new hermeneutic" (cf. Fuchs [1964]),
Gnosticism (cf. Robinson [1982]), doctrinal interests
(cf. Keck [1971), or some other arena in which Jesus
as an object of faith, in consequence of the Gospels,
rather than Jesus as the subject of faith, informing
the Gospels, is the principal concern. In other words,
"the new quest" became -- and remains -- so utterly

bound up with ideological programs, that it would be truer to say that it has never really been tried, than to say it has failed. Be that as it may, the period since the war has brought no significant advance in the study of Jesus.

The suggested itinerary of "the new quest" may someday be revived; whether or not it is, something needs to be done about the question of Jesus. For our present purpose, however, that question is not to be investigated in its properly historical or theological dimensions, since the essentially literary issue of how the Gospels unfolded is our purview. It may be that one's address of the literary issue will influence one's historical and/or theological judgment, and vice versa, but such influence is not our interest here; certainly, such questions can only be confused by muddling them, as they tend to be in "the new quest." Our concern is simply: what do we need to posit, as performed meaning within early Judaism, in order to explain how the Gospels came to say what they do? The answer to that question is the literary figure called Jesus, insofar as that figure can be known. (Once that figure is collated with historical evidence and reason, it may itself be claimed to be historical. But any such claim is not part of our inquiry.) To a significant extent, that figure is a cipher, an inference from texts. And yet the inference is not idle, since without that figure, the texts have no center, and cease to mean anything: they point to Jesus, not only denotatively, as their necessary precedent, but implicitly, as the informing source of what they mean. To this extent, it is sensible to speak of Jesus as a figure of literary history, whatever one might think of "the historical Jesus."

If Jesus' performance of the saying concerning foxes, birds, and the son of the man itself focused on the twin issues of christology and discipleship, that would certainly seem to explain the presentations of Matthew and Luke. But two considerations make that apparently straightforward explanation appear improbable. First, although there is a consensus between Matthew and Luke that the saying issues a call to discipleship grounded in christology, their respective understandings of both discipleship and christology are -- as we have seen -- distinctive. Were Jesus' performance explicitly geared to specific views of such central matters, greater fidelity to his perspective might be expected. Second, the reference to "the son of the man," cognate with that of Simeon ben Yohai, contrasts the genre of humanity with animate creation; such a usage is scarcely a straightforward vehicle of christology (or of messianic claims). Moreover, the point of the imagerial contrast pivots around the axis which separates people from animals, not disciples from rabble.

The performance of Jesus seems rather to have focused on how people are more rootless than animals. It inverts the logic of Simeon, his near contemporary. Where Simeon invoked the contrast between people and birds to show much more God would care for humanity, and therefore Simeon himself, Jesus used the same contrast to show how much more difficult life was for people, and therefore for Jesus himself, than it was for animals. The transformation of that performance in Matthew and Luke only makes sense if (a) "the son of the man" is taken christologically, and (b) rootlessness is related to discipleship in particular. In other words, their transformation of Jesus' aphorism, a harmless -- if somewhat cynical -- gnomon, is only tenable within the confessional and sociological environment of early Christianity.

The recovery of Jesus' performance, as an inference from and within the Gospels, is perfectly practicable, provided certain criteria are observed. To justify a characterization as "performance," a saying must proceed from an initiating figure of literary history, such as Simeon or Jesus, and that speaker must use the language of his milieu distinctively. In the present instance, their statements about "(the) son of (the) man" must be mutually intelligible, as they indeed are, but not merely repetitious. A remarkably obtuse school of criticism, represented recently by P. S. Alexander, complains that *any* attempt to describe Jesus' creativity is a veiled conspiracy to abstract him from Judaism (Alexander [1985] 242). Alexander would apparently revert to the school of pseudo-history, whose mantra is that there is nothing new under the sun. All is a matter of permutations and combinations within some classic core of meanings. For Alexander, the classic deposit is early Judaism, but it might as well be the New Testament, the Talmud, Thomas Aquinas, or the wisdom of the Reverend Moon. Obscurantists have at one time or another invoked all of those authorities, and many more, in an attempt to reduce the world of human meaning to the circle of writings whose interpretation they regulate. Despite every systematic attempt to weed out notions of creativity and distinctiveness, the fact is that significantly literary figures are held by the literatures which refer to them to say and do things which are understood to be important. They say and do surprising things, which influence the perceived course of events, and neither the performers nor what they performed would be recalled otherwise. Of course Jesus performed within early Judaism, as did Simeon; but neither can be reduced to a repetition of the other. And the irony is, that neither performance is accessible directly from a source of early Judaism, although both are located in tributaries thereof: Jesus' saying is conveyed in Gospels, Simeon's in Talmud and Midrash. There is much that is new under the sun.

TEMPTATIONS AND NIGHTS

The examples of the first three Studies suggest that, in their material synopticity, the Gospels are not odd developments within early Judaism. The relative degrees of expansion, abbreviation, intercalation, and addition vary among the texts that have been considered, but at no point did our examples from Rabbinica appear incomparable. Just that finding, however, only serves to underscore an evident disanalogy between the two sets of synoptic relationship, as so far surveyed. Whatever may be said of their material synopticity, the taxic synopticity of the first three Gospels, their comparability in their ordering of pericopae, sets them apart from rabbinic analogies which are in other respects instructive.

The potential importance of the Targumim in this connection will be immediately obvious. It may be argued that the Targumim require special attention on other grounds, in that their design is suited to usage in synagogue, rather than academy (cf. Chilton [1986] 113), that is, they were framed to hand on and interpret the Law, Prophets, and Writings for the purposes of public worship. Sociologically, such a function may be closer to that of the Gospels than are, say, Talmud and Midrash, which are formally intended more for professional discussion than for public instruction. More crucially for the present purpose, Targumim evince both taxic and material synopticity. In principle, they were oral: the meturgeman was forbidden to consult a text as he translated, lest there be any confusion between the paraphrase and the written canon in the mind of the congregation (cf. Megillah 32a). Whatever the practice in the synagogue, the Targumim did come to be fixed in writing, and that froze their wording at a moment of their development in a way which has permitted posterity to consider their formation. The Hebrew text is the primary datum of all Targumim, to which they consistently do justice (cf. Koch [1972]), but they also deviate from that written tradition for the sake of clarity or exposition (cf. Stenning's introduction

[1949]). The workings of the process are particularly
apparent in the case of Pentateuchal Targumim, where
we can compare several renderings of the same Hebrew
corpus. Among these Targumim (especially those styled
Palestinian) we have verbatim agreements and marked
deviations; Martin McNamara has rightly observed, "we
do have a synoptic problem" (McNamara [1972] 168).

　　The more famous synoptic problem in the New
Testament presents an obvious possible analogy, and
all the more so as at least a restricted period of
oral transmission must be postulated in respect of
dominical tradition. Certain aspects of oral
transmission have been invoked to solve "the Synoptic
Problem," as has been mentioned in the Introduction.
J. M. Rist's recent study resuscitates the hypothesis
of an oral gospel to explain the relationship between
Matthew and Mark (1978), but just what was this oral
gospel like? Various models have been suggested. Form
criticism gave us pericopae -- discrete pearls
threaded on a redactional string by the "Evangelists,"
and each pearl a formation of the community over (at
best) a dominical piece of sand (cf. Kümmel [1973]
327-338). Thorleif Boman (1967) has attacked this
model, showing quite convincingly from the orally
developed literature of many cultures that we must
think rather of longer, continuous epics at the point
of origin which were woven together over the course of
time. The evident weakness in Boman's analogy is that
the gospel of Jesus was not preached in some
anthropological abstract, but -- in the first instance
-- in a specifically Jewish culture. Birger
Gerhardsson (1961) has shown how much might be learned
from that fact and has used the Mishnah as a model for
understanding the development of the New Testament.
But Morton Smith (1963) has rightly complained against
Gerhardsson that, in addition to being quite late,
Mishnah is too specialist, to the point of being *sui
generis*, to be of direct relevance in understanding
the formation of the New Testament. Targumim, however,
provide a possible analogy for four reasons, (1) they
are oral in one sense and written in another, (2) they
are specifically Jewish, (3) they are designed for

popular consumption, and (4) they manifest a synoptic relationship.

The fourth dimension of possible analogy between the Synoptic Gospels and the Palestinian Targumim requires special attention. The Targumic "synoptic problem" of which McNamara speaks is both material and taxic. Precisely because the function of the Targumim is to render scripture, that additional level of analogy with the Synoptics (notably absent from other forms of Rabbinica), stereotyped order, is operative. As a test case, to assess the possible analogy further, it is proposed to compare the Synoptic story of Jesus' temptation with "the Poem of the Four Nights" in the Palestinian Targumim. These passages are chosen because they are each self-contained, and because both are constructed from scriptural citations and allusions. (N.b., the Poem refers to more than Exodus 12:42, of which it is the putative rendering). It is to be stressed that any literary dependence between the Targumim and the Synoptic Gospels forms no part of our argument; their qualitative difference in subject matter immediately precludes such an implication. Moreover, the reference to the Aqedah in the Poem seems quite late, as I have argued elsewhere (cf. Chilton [1980]). We are attending to the simple task of asking whether the structure of these passages and the alterations which occur through their transmissions might justify the claim that Synoptic tradition is comparable with Targumic tradition, and -- if so -- to what extent it may be said to be comparable.

A consideration of the Poem as found in the Fragments Targum will show the structural importance of scriptural references, of which the most major are identified in brackets:

> It is a night to be observed and set aside for redemption before the LORD when he brought forth the sons of Israel, freed from the land of Egypt. Because four nights are written in the book of memorials.

[The "watching" of the LORD and of Israel on this night is already mentioned in Exodus 12:42 within the Masoretic Text.]

The first night, when the LORD's memra was revealed upon the world to create it, when the world was without form and void and darkness was spread on the face of the deep, and the LORD's memra illuminated and enlightened; he called it the first night.

[Genesis 1:1-5, quite obviously, paraphrased, one might note (given that "memra" might be translated as "word"), in a manner reminiscent of the Johannine prologue.]

The second night, when the LORD's memra was revealed upon Abraham between the parts. Abraham was a hundred years old and Sarah was ninety years old, to establish what scripture says, is Abraham, a hundred years old, able to beget, and is Sarah, ninety years old, able to bear? Was not Isaac our father thirty-seven years old at the time he was offered on the altar? The heavens descended and came down and Isaac saw their perfections and his eyes were darkened from the heights, and he called it the second night.

[The second night is identified with various moments in the history of salvation, arranged in a sequential pattern: Abraham's covenant sacrifice (Genesis 15:17), the removal of the obstacle to the covenant promise (Genesis 17:17), and the confirmation of the promise in respect of Isaac (Genesis 22:1-18 cf. 27:1). Isaac's age is also generated midrashically, from the notice immediately after chapter 22 that Sarah was 127 years old (23:1).]

The third night, when the LORD's memra was revealed upon the Egyptians at the dividing of the night; his right hand killed the first born of the Egyptians and his right hand spared the

first born of Israel, to establish what scripture
says, Israel is my first born son, and he called
it the third night.

[Primarily, this refers to Exodus 12:29, cf. vv.
12, 13, 23, 27 and 4:22.]

The fourth night, when the end of the age is
accomplished to be redeemed, the servants of
wickedness are destroyed and the iron yokes
broken. Moses comes from the desert, but the king
messiah from above. One leads in the head of the
cloud, and the other leads in the head of the
cloud, and the LORD's memra leads them both, and
they will go together.

This is the night of passover before the LORD, to
be observed and set aside by the sons of Israel
in their generations.

[Eventually, we get back to Exodus 12:42, but the
eschatology of Moses and the messiah is not
biblical in the same sense that the references
included in the texts attached to the first three
nights are. (M. L. Klein has defended the
superiority of reading "flock," instead of
"cloud;" but I have questioned that judgment in a
review of *Geniza Manuscripts of Palestinian
Targum* (1986; cf. Chilton [1988]). The point in
any case does not feature crucially in the
present argument.)]

While Neophyti's Poem does deviate from this version,
its most striking feature is its similarity to the
Poem as we have cited it (cf. Appendix IV).
   The Fragments Targum's Poem obviously differs
signally from the Matthean temptation. The Targum
opens and closes with a reference to the Hebrew text
it renders, while Matthew refers first to the
temptation by the devil (4:1) and finally to the
support of the angels (4:11). Structurally, Matthew
presents a three-tiered dialogue or repartee between
biblical passages as spoken by the principals, while

the Targum straightforwardly offers the reader
biblical exposition of the four nights. But two
significant similarities should be observed at the
outset. First, in each, a clearly associative chain
links the citations. The LORD's memra is a primary
agency in each Targumic explication of the nights. The
Matthean interplay of citations centers on the proper
place of the "son" in relation to God. Second, the
climactic point in both (in the Targum, the haggadah
of Moses and the messiah, in Matthew, the devil's
invitation to apostasy) is not directly a biblical
citation, but is immediately followed by one.
Curiously, the climax of both is at the point furthest
distant from scripture. The structural patterns of
these two very different passages are therefore
distinctive, and yet they are similar enough to hint
at the possibility that they were transmitted in a
comparable manner.

When we turn to Luke's temptation, we see
another structural similarity to the Targumic Poem:
Luke opens and closes (4:2, 13) with a reference to
the devil's tempting, which is treated as if it were
the primary datum to be explicated, the "text." The
Lukan order, however, insures that the pattern of a
climactic departure from scripture is broken. But this
may not be used as evidence that Luke here disrupts
any analogy to Targumic transmission. On the contrary,
variations in order are well known to students of the
Targumim, and two instances may be cited in respect of
the Poem: (1) in Neophyti, which generally follows the
Fragments Targum more closely than Luke follows
Matthew, the reference to Exodus 4:22 ("his first born
son is Israel"), which the Fragments Targum cites in
the context of the third night, is attached in the
margin to the second night, (2) the ancient midrash on
Exodus, Mekhilta de R. Simeon b. Yoḥai, actually
presents a poem of three nights, omitting the
messianic fourth night (cf. Le Déaut [1963] 151 n.
50). The Lukan alteration appears median between the
slighter change of Neophyti (margin) and the radical
excision of the Mekhilta (which also, of course, omits
the departure from directly scriptural reference
altogether).

The Markan compression of the temptation (relatively speaking) into two verses (1:12, 13) is so stark as to suggest to some scholars that it does not come from the same stable as the "Q" account (cf. Taylor [1952] and Cranfield [1959]). But the relation of Mark to Matthew and Luke in this matter is perhaps more explicable when we compare the following version of the Poem, from Targum Pseudo-Jonathan, to those of the Fragments Targum and Neophyti:

Four nights are written in the book of memorials before the Lord of the world. The first night, when he was revealed to create the world; the second night, when he was revealed upon Abraham; the third night, when he was revealed against Egypt, his left hand killing all the first born of Egypt and his right hand sparing the first born of Israel; the fourth night, when he will be revealed to redeem the people of the house of Israel from among the nations....

It is true that the version in Pseudo-Jonathan at least maintains the structure of four nights, while Mark does not do any justice to the three specific temptations, and that there is little new in Pseudo-Jonathan as compared to the Fragments Targum and Neophyti, while the beasts mentioned by Mark constitute an odd deviation from Matthew and Luke. But all that having been said, the fact remains that the scriptural references in the Poem as found in Pseudo-Jonathan are so attenuated as to be nearly non-existent, the second night passage lacks a reference to Isaac, and the passage of the fourth night is no longer explicitly messianic. The analogy to Mark in relation to its colleagues is certainly not exact, but it is also not entirely uninstructive.

Literal agreement and frustrating variety in diction pose a major difficulty to theories of documentary dependence. Why should Mark follow his scroll of Matthew verbatim (or vice versa) in one passage and pick up a different scroll when he comes to write another? Even if it is credible that the "Evangelists" had libraries at their disposal, why

should an author use a predecessor's material when
writing up a passage and then, before he gets to the
end, suddenly go his own way by adding, deleting,
abbreviating, expanding, conflating, separating,
and/or changing its context? "Literal agreement" is
still used as the trump card by those who argue
literary dependence, but the latter is not a necessary
inference from the former. The relationship between
the Fragments Targum and Neophyti already suggests
that documents which were oral in origin -- and were
always so in principle -- might agree literally. But
the phenomenon in the Synoptic Gospels for which we
are seeking an analogy is agreement and variety
together; for this reason, we may leave Mark and
Pseudo-Jonathan aside, because both documents present
the passages in question in such a relatively
compressed form that they are idiosyncratic from the
point of view of the words they employ. We are
therefore left to compare Matthew and Luke, on the one
hand, with the Fragments Targum and Neophyti, on the
other.

The present inquiry does not require that we
observe all the variations manifest in the two sets of
documents. We will restrict ourselves to selecting a
sample of substantive deviations between Matthew and
Luke, and then see whether or not analogous deviations
can be found between the Fragments Targum and
Neophyti. Because we use one of a pair of documents as
our starting point for collation, we will speak of its
partner as "changing" or "adding" or "omitting" words,
but such language is only used as a convenience in
order to describe the linguistic relations at issue,
not as an assertion of literary or oral priority. The
deviations between Matthew and Luke selected for
analysis are as follows:

1.   Luke 4:1 (cf. Matthew 4:1) adds "Full of the
holy spirit he returned from the Jordan."

2.   Luke 4:2 (cf. Matthew 4:2) adds "And he ate
nothing in those days and when they were ended he
hungered."

3.   Luke 4:3 (cf. Matthew 4:3) changes "the tempter" to "the devil" and "these stones" (nominative) to "this stone" (dative).

4.   Luke 4:4 (cf. Matthew 4:4) omits "but by every word proceeding from God's mouth."

5.   Luke 4:5, 6 (cf. Matthew 4:8, 9) adds "in a moment of time" and "for it is given to me and to whom I wish to give it."

6.   Luke 4:13 (cf. Matthew 4:11) omits "And behold angels came and ministered to him."

As will be seen, each of the deviations selected is distinctive from the others, so we are not considering a mere multiplication of the same sort of variant. Each deviation will be described briefly, and a Targumic analogue posited.

Deviations and their Analogues

Deviation 1 is of a narrative order, linking the Lukan temptation to the baptism (3:21, 22). The resumptive clause is appropriate, serving to take the story line up again after the long, parenthetical genealogy (3:23-38). In Analogue 1, the Fragments Targum adds "between the parts" to the beginning of the second night passage. This serves to specify Genesis 15:17 as the relevant allusion. Of course, this is not as substantial an addition as Luke's, the purpose is to fix the second night exegetically, rather than geographically or chronologically, and it may be argued that Neophyti implies the allusion already. Nonetheless, the fact remains that, at the beginning of a passage, the Fragments Targum augments the narrative content relative to Neophyti.

Deviation 2 is also narrative, but its purpose is to explain the course of events more fully than Matthew's "afterward he hungered" does. In Analogue 2 where, in the first night passage, the Fragments Targum reads "the LORD's memra illuminated and enlightened," Neophyti has "the LORD's memra was light," thereby explicating the scene in terms of Genesis 1:3. (Alternatively, the Fragments Targum might be considered to fill out a bare scriptural reference in more narrative terms.) Again, the Targumic addition is less fulsome than Luke's, and it explicates the Poem in respect of scripture, not event. But it must be borne in mind that the meturgeman's text was the written word, while the Evangelist's "text" was Jesus, and that the Poem is less susceptible of narrative embellishment than is a haggadic story.

Deviation 3 is a simple case of preferred idioms used of the same referent. *Analogue* 3 manifests a definite pattern: in each of the three cases (in the first, second and third night texts) where Neophyti speaks of the LORD being revealed, the Fragments Targum meticulously refers to the LORD's "memra." Similarly, in the prologue and epilogue to the Poem, Neophyti says the night is remembered "to the name of the LORD," while the Fragments Targum simply has "before the LORD."

Deviation 4 instances an abbreviated citation of a biblical passage, and it is interesting that Luke's comparative lacuna is filled in by many manuscripts. *Analogue* 4 within the Poem in Pseudo-Jonathan actually presents the nearest such instance, but it has already been pointed out that Neophyti omits the reference to Genesis 15:17 (see *Analogue* 1). Without "between the parts" the second night might be thought of as referring simply to Genesis 17 and 18. The sphere of ideas remains the same, but the precise allusions do vary somewhat between the Fragments Targum and Neophyti.

Deviation 5 is again essentially narrative, but it performs a dramatic function in emphasizing the devil's power. *Analogue* 5 occurs in the passage of the fourth night, where the Fragments Targum explicitly refers to the messiah, but Neophyti does not. While Moses and messiah appear on clouds in the Fragments Targum, Moses and the (so far unidentified) figure in Neophyti lead the flock. This complex of variants is more important than may at first appear, because Neophyti then has the second figure speak as "I", presumably an allusion to God himself. (Interestingly, the speaker is אנא ("I") and leads the עאנא ("flock"); the pattern within Neophyti appears conscious. That is another reason to be cautious in respect of reading "flock" in the Fragments Targum [cf. Klein (1978) and the earlier reference to criticism of his proposal].) This adjustment in reference is a more extreme development than the change from Matthew to Luke, but the Fragments Targum does present a more balanced portrayal of the dramatis personae.

Deviation 6 is the sole alteration in Luke which constitutes a significant omission. Analogue 6 has already been mentioned (see Analogue 5): Neophyti simply deletes "and the king messiah from above" from the text of the fourth night.

At several points we have already had to acknowledge that the analogues posited are defective. Where it is a question of narrative deviation (see 1, 2, 5), the Gospels appeared to embellish the temptation, while the Targumim in two out of three of those cases (1, 2) merely added a biblical reference or made the reference more explicit. The difference in procedure may tell us more about the distinction between Targum and Euanggelion in respect of purpose than about any qualitative difference in the manner in which they were transmitted. Analogues 1 and 2 are, it is true, rather more restrained than Deviations 1 and 2, but the evidence we have considered prevents us from saying that Targumic transmission was more conservative than Evangelical transmission. Deviation-Analogue 5 would overturn such a generalization: the Targumic variation in defining the second figure in the text of the fourth night is more radical than the Evangelical shift in emphasis on the devil's power. The extent of the change in the Targumic text is further indicated by the fact that the same text presents the closest analogy to Deviation 6, where Luke drops an important element of the temptation. Deviation-Analogue 4 is also not very exact, curiously because the Gospels of Matthew and Luke are more extensive and precise in their biblical citation than the Targumim in question are at this particular point.   Deviation-Analogue 3 is

unquestionably the best of the lot, and it is surely
of interest to the student of the Gospels that these
Targumim present a pattern of distinct but practically
synonymous expression -- the very linguistic
relationship which lies at the heart of "the Synoptic
Problem."

When dictional agreements and disagreements
among the Targumic Poems are considered in comparison
with the Synoptic temptation, and one bears in mind
how similar the Poem appears to the temptation in its
structure and variations of order and size, the
possibility does emerge that the Gospels may have
taken shape according to a process cognate with that
which produced the Targumim. The example analysis
suggests that the possibility might be used as a
hypothesis for treating more material of different
types. Both the temptation and the Poem are basically
sui generis within the documents within which they
appear; a representative sampling from the major
strata of the Gospels and the Targumim would have to
be dealt with in this way, and similar results to
those achieved in the present study obtained, before
the hypothesis here suggested could justifiably be
called a thesis. Nonetheless, we do have before us a
possibility which might warrant such further research.
At the level of their material synopticity, the
Palestinian Targumim are potentially at least as
illuminating of the Synoptic Gospels as are other
sorts of Rabbinica.

For those seeking the appropriate focus for
future research, the analysis here conducted suggests
certain warnings. Quite obviously, nothing we have
observed in the temptation as compared to the Poem
should incline us to describe the Gospels as a species
of Targum. On the contrary, our consideration of
dictional disagreements which are narrative
(*Deviations* 1, 2, 5) plainly showed that these
embellishments on the story line, specifying Jesus'
attitude and position in the proceedings and the power
of the devil he faced, were of a different order from
the exegetical notes and haggadic digressions added in
the Fragments Targum and Neophyti. The goal of
Targumim is to provide an understanding of a written

text, while Gospels are designed to explain the significance of a person. The "text" of the Evangelists was Jesus, and as soon as we have said that, we realize that it is meaningless to say the Gospels are Targumic in form, even though they occasionally cite Targumic renderings (so Harris [1920-21] 373-376 and McNamara [1972] 169). Nor is the distinction between Targum and Gospel merely formal: each form is congruent with the purpose of its genre, and the Targumim interpret a text as consistently as the Gospels interpret a person. It follows that the processes which produced Targumim and Gospels should not be confused, because the controlling influence on one process is (consciously) textual while the controlling influence on the other is (again, consciously) personal. For this reason, I speak of the two processes as being "cognate" rather than "identical," and of the similarities between the two as "analogues," not "parallels."

If these processes are cognate, then the Targumim give us a handle for grasping the interplay between tradition and interpretation in the Gospels. When the meturgeman arose in the synagogue to translate, his duty was twofold: (1) he had to do justice to the biblical text in Hebrew which he was to render in Aramaic, but (2) he was also obliged to look away from any text, to face the congregation and in so doing to explain what had been read in terms the congregation could appropriate. At times these two ends could seem to be in tension, as for example in the case of the question of how Exodus 24:10 should be rendered. The Hebrew text is: "and they saw the God of Israel." This was impossible in the contemporary understanding, so perhaps one should say "and they saw the angel of the God of Israel." R. Judah condemned both renderings in his famous and paradoxical dictum (Kiddushin 49a; cf. the discussion in McNamara [1972] 41):

> If one translates a verse literally, he is a liar; if he adds thereto, he is a blasphemer and a libeler.

In the same Talmudic passage, Onqelos ("our Targum")
is authorized as normative: "Then what is meant by
translation? Our translation." And Onqelos solves the
problem:

and they saw the glory of the God of Israel.

"Glory" is not an addition in the sense that "angel"
is, because God is not replaced with another figure;
at the same time, the lie that God is visible to men
is not perpetrated. (Cf. Exodus 33:18-23, where both
God's invisibility to mortals, and the available of
his glory, are explicit.) The authority of a Targum
resides in its care for tradition (sc. the text and
the efforts of earlier translators), but not only in
that; the other constituent of its authority is its
adequacy as a statement about the God referred to in
the text.

     Such interplay between tradition and redaction
is easily instanced in the Gospels. The portrayal of
Jesus which we see in them is definitely conditioned
by the traditions about him which were available, but
these traditions are selected and shaped in the course
of transmission (both at the traditional and the
redactional levels). A single example will perhaps
suffice to illustrate. In the controversy centered on
the man with a withered hand (Matthew 12:9-14; Mark
3:1-6; Luke 6:6-11), Jesus confronts his opponents
with a saying (about doing good on the Sabbath; vv.
12, 4, 9 respectively) and an action (the healing; vv.
13, 5, 10). The attitude of the opponents is clear:
they wish to find a reason to accuse Jesus (vv. 10, 2,
7). But what was the attitude of Jesus himself? In
what seems an early characterization of his attitude,
Mark 3:5a presents Jesus "looking round at them with
anger, grieved at their hardness of heart." Luke
eschews this affective language: Jesus merely fixes
them with a stare ("looking round at them all") and
performs the healing which causes *them* to be "filled
with fury" (6:10a, 11). Matthew has no reference to
emotion on either side in the two corresponding verses
(12:13, 14), but pursues its characteristic tendency
of letting dialogue alone tell the tale (cf. Held

[1963], in the volume he produced with Bornkamm and Barth). Slight changes of diction, such as we have seen in the passages concerning Jesus' temptation and their Targumic analogies, manifest distinctive emphases in the portrayal of Jesus. The Markan Christ is consumed with the acute emotions which almost force him to behave as he does; the Lukan Lord is the master of the situations that confront him; the Matthean Son is best characterized by the words and deeds he himself provides as teaching. The Church which authorized these portraits of Jesus, and many others, by including them in its canon attested not only to their value as tradition, but to their efficacy as interpretations which illuminated Jesus' person for believers. The integrity of such tradition was not a strait-jacket which forced tradents of the gospel into merely mechanical transmission; the paramount concern was rather for the significance of tradition for faith, so that explication was as much a part of the authority of these books as their incorporation of previous data.

"Oral tradition" is widely posited as the medium of the gospel's transmission between the resurrection and our written Gospels, largely on the argument *faute de mieux* that something of the kind must have taken place during that period. The insecurity felt by many at the notion that the facts about Jesus should have been handed down in this fashion is inevitable, despite the familiarity we all have with the howlers to which the written word is liable, since "writing" and "accuracy" are so closely allied in our culture. Birger Gerhardsson's contribution (1961) has reminded us that this was not the case in the New Testament period, and unease has been somewhat allayed. By way of summary, we might contrast our findings with those of Gerhardsson's thesis. He has suggested that mishnaic transmission, in which the opinions of various rabbis were recorded with a view to their relevance in legal controversies, might be a model for understanding the pre-written history of our Gospels. As was already discussed, Morton Smith has reminded us that the Mishnah is simply too late (in comparison with the New Testament) to supply us with an immediate

model for Jewish oral tradition in the first century.
And we must stress again that the Mishnah is
essentially a tool for rabbinic discussion, not a
catechetical document for popular use. These
objections vitiate Gerhardsson's thesis, and they must
be answered before it is appealed to as a support for
the "authenticity" of the Gospels' tradition as a
whole. Further, we might point out that Jesus'
disciples obviously did not transmit his sayings as
those of the rabbis in Mishnah. Mishnah presents a
collection of sayings from various sages (cf. Viviano
[1978]), but the early Christians never handed on
dominical logia as if their significance lay in their
relationship to the assertions of others. From the
collectors who first brought together the sayings
which we know from the Synoptic Gospels to the Coptic
Gospel according to Thomas, what Jesus had to say was
seen to have divine authorization. Indeed, Christians
ultimately went so far as to take the audacious step
(from a conservatively religious point of view) of
adding something they called the New Testament to
scripture. They saw the words and deeds of Jesus as
having a status comparable -- and ultimately
equivalent -- to that of Moses and the prophets.

With this in mind, I see nothing inappropriate
in the claim that the disciples might have used
Targumic methods to transmit the words and deeds of
Jesus. They were certainly important enough to them to
merit such treatment, and our observation of synoptic
analogies between the Palestinian Targumim and the
first three Gospels suggests that they may actually
have received such treatment. Of course (once again)
we must always bear in mind that Targumim are
essentially Aramaic paraphrases of Hebrew texts, while
the Gospels are expositions of Jesus' life, death and
resurrection which only occasionally (and largely
inferentially) translate Semitic locutions. The
evidence permits of no confusion between Targumim and
Gospels, but it also intimates that the latter were
handed down by the use of procedures which were
developed in connection with the former. Our
suggestion is not that the Gospels are Targumim, but
that the Gospels took shape in much the same way that

Targumim did. The extant Palestinian Targumim are quite late, but the process of Targumic formation is agreed to be primitive in origin. (Pseudo-Jonathan is now agreed to be post-Islamic [no earlier than the seventh century], and an emerging consensus would place Neophyti I in the third century, perhaps near the time that Onqelos substantively emerged; the Fragments Targum may be dated to the ninth century, if not later. Nonetheless, Targumic traditions have been identified within the Gospels, cf. McNamara [1972] and Chilton, *Rabbi* [1984]. As in the case of other forms of rabbinic literature, then, documents of varying dates are sometimes more comparable in wording than the Gospels are.) Just as the present suggestion is not as sensitive as Gerhardsson's when the question of dating is raised, so it fares better when we recall that, unlike Mishnah, the Targumim belonged to the people in the synagogues as well as to the experts in the academy. The disciples of Jesus, as participants in synagogues, would have had first-hand knowledge of such sacred, oral tradition: that knowledge, it seems, was an important resource to them as they tried to transmit the words and deeds of Jesus.

Their choice of a medium, no doubt more reflexive than deliberate, evidences their apparently immediate appreciation that the words and deeds of Jesus were of the order of the words and deeds of the God of scripture, and were accordingly to be handed down by a method akin to that used by the meturgemanin. In other words, the taxic synopticity of the Gospels is itself a clue of the sort of materials disciples felt they were handling: they behaved as if the halakhah and haggadah of Jesus were akin to scripture. Tradition and interpretation were the proper means of making what God had once done comprehensible, and were now embraced and developed to announce what it was that God had done in the case of Jesus.

BEELZEBUL AND CAIN -- CASES OF DEVIATION

The previous study delineated four sorts of analogy
between the Targumic presentation of the Poem of the
Four Nights and the Synoptic presentation of Jesus'
temptation:

> (1) the structural centrality of citations from
> the Hebrew scriptures, carefully related to one
> another;

> (2) variations in order between one version of
> the passage and another;

> (3) the radical brevity of one version as
> compared with the others;

> (4) six types of linguistic deviation among both
> the Targums and the Gospels against a background
> of verbatim similarity.

The evidence considered was in line with the
investigation of material synopticity by other
Targumists (cf. Grelot [1959], Kuiper [1970, 1972],
Vermes [1960-61]).

In order to pursue the possibility that the two
synoptic relationships might be cognate, and might
therefore reflect a common medium of development,
another test case is here offered. In the instance of
the temptation, triple tradition is in question, and
the relationship between Mark and the so-called "Q"
material is problematic. A Synoptic passage was
therefore sought in which Markan material is
paralleled rather exactly in Matthew and Luke, and in
which Matthew and Luke "add" tradition commonly
designated as "Q." Accordingly, the Beelzebul
controversy (Matthew 12:22-30/Mark 3:22-27/Luke
11:14-23) was selected. For several reasons, the
debate between Cain and Abel, reported in the
Palestinian Targums at Genesis 4:8, seemed a good
candidate for comparison with the Beelzebul pericope.
Both complexes of passages are controversial
dialogues, both involve substantive elaborations in

some versions as contrasted to a single, briefer
version, and both manifest the attempt to coordinate
the material presented so as to achieve theological
consistency.

Four versions of the dispute between Cain and
Abel appear in four Targums whose dates are uncertain;
indeed the very method by which dates should be
assigned to our documents is a matter for discussion.
The Cairo Geniza fragments are commonly dated
according to the period of their manuscripts (between
the seventh century and the fifteenth century), while
the medieval attestation of Ms Neophyti I has not
prevented its ascription to a much earlier period on
theological grounds; Pseudo-Jonathan is said to be
post-Islamic on the basis of its latest identifiable
historical allusion, but the Fragments Targum, as its
designation suggests, is not extensive enough to be
susceptible of such analysis and so escapes a late
dating at the hands of a minority of scholars, despite
the fact that its manuscript attestation is also
medieval. In the absence of a coherent method for
establishing the dates and proveniences of these
obviously related documents, the Palestinian Targums
should be taken as evidencing -- in the main, given
their clear affinity with Rabbinica -- interpretative
activity in the Amoraic period (cf. Schäfer [1980]).
Whatever the prehistory of each Targum, the linguistic
similarity between them in forming a middle term
between the Aramaic of Qumran, Onqelos and Jonathan on
the one hand, and that of the Palestinian Talmud on
the other, would suggest that the Palestinian Targums
achieved their recognizable form during a single
period (that is, in the third and fourth centuries)
and did not emerge sporadically, although the
emergence of several of them as texts was obviously
gradual (cf. Grelot [1959] 86).

The substantive agreement between the
Palestinian Targumim at Genesis 4:8 suits the
hypothesis sketched above. But neither our hypothesis,
nor any comprehensive theory of how these Targums are
related, permits us to say which of them, if any, is
the "source" of another. To speak of "sources" may
itself be misleading in any case, given that -- as

used in synagogue worship -- Targums were always oral in principle. Yet we can proceed to characterize the Targums in terms of one another, once the texts themselves are set out (cf. Appendix 5; the typographical format of the presentation here will be explained in the "Comparative Analysis"), bearing in mind that we are in no position to conclude that one is literarily prior to another.

THE TEXTS

CAIRO GENIZA

> I Cain answered and said to Abel,
> I see that the world is created with mercies,
> and it is led with mercies:
> [----------------] for what reason
> was your offering received from you with favor
> and it was not received from me with favor?

> II Abel answered and said to Cain,
> what if the world is created with mercies
> and it is led with mercies? It is still led with fruits of good deeds:
> because my deeds were more correct than yours
> my offering was received from me with favor
> and from you it was not received with favor.

PSEUDO-JONATHAN

> (A) I Cain answered and said to Abel,
> I know that the world is created with mercies,
> but it is not led according to fruits of good deeds,
> and there is favoritism of persons in judgment:
> for what reason

> was your offering received
> and my offering not received from me with
>   favor?

   II   Abel answered and said to Cain,
>   the world is created with mercies,
>   and it is led according to fruits of good
>   deeds,
>   and there is no favoritism of persons in
>   judgment:
>   and because the fruits of my deeds surpassed
>   yours
>   -- and were more timely than yours --
>   my offering was received with favor.

(B) I   Cain answered and said to Abel,
>   there is no judgment and there is no judge,
>   and there is no other world,
>   and there is no giving of good reward
>   to the righteous
>   and there is no repaying from the wicked.

   II   Abel answered and said to Cain,
>   there is judgment and there is a judge,
>   and there is another world,
>   and there is giving good reward to the
>   righteous
>   and there is repaying from the wicked.

NEOPHYTI I

(A) I   Cain answered and said to Abel,
>   I know the world is not created with mercies,
>   and it is not led in respect of fruits of
>   good deeds,
>   and there is accepting of persons in
>   judgment:
>   for what reason
>   was your offering received with favor
>   and my offering was not received from me with
>   favor?

II Abel answered and said to Cain,
    I know the world is created with mercies,
    and in respect of fruits of good deeds it is
        led:
    and because my good deeds surpassed yours
    my offering was received from me with favor
    while your offering was not received
        from you with favor.

(B) I Cain answered and said to Abel,
        there is no judgment and there is no judge,
        and there is no other world,
        there is no giving good reward to the
            righteous
        and there is no repaying from the wicked.

    II Abel answered and said to Cain,
        there is judgment and there is a judge,
        and there is another world,
        and there is giving good reward to the
            righteous
        and there is repaying from the wicked
            in the world to come.

FRAGMENTS TARGUM

(B) I Cain answered and said to Abel,
        there is no judgment and there is no judge,
        and there is no other world,
        and there is no giving good reward to the
            righteous
        and no repaying from the wicked:

(A) I and the world is not created with mercies
        and it is not led with mercies:
            for what reason
        was your offering received from you with favor
        and from me it was not received with favor?

(B) II Abel answered and said to Cain,
         there is judgment and there is a judge,
         and there is another world,

and there is giving good reward to the
   righteous
and repaying from the wicked;

(A) II and the world is created with mercies
      and it is led with mercies. It is still led
         according to fruits of good deeds:
      because the fruits of my deeds surpassed yours
      my offering was received from me with favor
      and from you it was not received with favor.

COMPARATIVE ANALYSIS

Cairo Geniza (hereafter: CG):

This is the simplest version of the basically similar
paraphrases of Genesis 4:8 in the Palestinian
Targumim. Cain charges that "mercies" determine God's
behavior. The implicit accusation is that his justice
is wanting: the entirely implicit nature of this
complaint is a distinguishing feature of CG Genesis
4:8 (which is why a lacuna is indicated after line 3).
Abel agrees the world is created with mercies, but
insists that "fruits of good deeds" are taken into
account by God and that God's sensitivity to these was
the basis on which his own offering was accepted in
preference to Cain's.

Pseudo-Jonathan (hereafter: PJ):

Relative to the simple version in CG, PJ presents an
elaboration of the wording and structure of the debate
between Cain and Abel. Cain's initial charge expressly
doubts the divine justice: favoritism, not "fruits of
good deeds" is said to occasion God's acceptance of
Abel's sacrifice. Abel explicitly denies the
accusation at each point, adding, in this version,
that his own deeds were better and more punctual than
Cain's. So far, we have described the elaboration
found in PJ as compared to CG in that part of the
Cain-Abel debate which is held in common by them. We
designate this part of the structure of the passage in

PJ Genesis 4:8 as "A" to distinguish it from what
follows. "B" in PJ is a substantive elaboration as
compared to CG: the debate is extended to cover
elements which are corollary to the denial or
affirmation of divine justice. If God is not just,
there is no theological basis on which to secure the
hope of divine retribution in the next world, and
Cain's next assault is in fact on such classical
theodicies as we find in 4 Ezra. Abel's reply is
perfectly symmetrical to Cain's attack, and suggests
that these specific affirmations are key tenets in the
mind of the meturgeman.

Neophyti I (hereafter: N):

The substantive structural agreement between N and PJ
is obvious, and N can be characterized in respect of
CG as much as PJ can be. The slight idiolectical
variations between PJ and N (cf. A.I, lines 3, 4, 5;
A.II, lines 2, 3-end) need not detain us, although N's
omission of Abel's explicit denial of favoritism and
of his insistence that his good deeds were timely is
significant. The omission permits the meturgeman of N
to devote more space, as compared to what we have in
PJ, to the statements of Cain and Abel regarding the
rejection or acceptance of their offerings: in this
regard, N follows CG, not PJ. But N departs from both
CG and PJ in having Cain deny the creation of the
world "with mercies" (A.I, 2), which is the very
premise of his attack in CG and PJ. The structure of
denial and affirmation has apparently influenced the
way in which the theological argument is presented to
the extent that this form determines N's content.

Fragments Targum (hereafter: FT):

FT presents a most complex and unusual version of the
dialogue, but it is nonetheless linguistically and
substantively comparable with the other Palestinian
Targumim. With N (and against CG and PJ), the creation
"with mercies" is denied by Cain, but so is government
"with mercies" (cf. CG): favoritism and fruits of good
deeds are not mentioned by him. That is, Cain in FT

simply negates what he says in CG. Moreover, the reply
of Abel to this charge (i.e., not to Cain's doubts
about theodicy) is also more similar to the CG version
than to the others, although Abel's insistence that
his deeds "surpassed" Cain's is more similar to PJ and
N than to CG. The stress on the sentence regarding the
respective offerings of Cain and Abel is more
reminiscent of CG and N than of PJ. The argument about
theodicy is presented in the terms of PJ and N, but
its placement gives this version of the debate as a
whole the most deviant structure among the Palestinian
Targums. The scheme of denial and affirmation in the
debate concerning theodicy has not only (as in N)
contaminated the diction of the theological debate,
but the order has been shuffled so as to give
precedence to the dispute about the judgment, the
judge, the other world and retribution. In the
speeches of both Cain and Abel a statement on this
subject is made first, and a theological assertion
(regarding the divine disposition in creating and
ordering the world) follows as subsidiary to it. The
simpler structure of CG is approximated (in that there
is only one denial and one response), but the
substantive innovation of N is brought to a radical
conclusion in FT.

As in the case of the synoptic relationship
among the first three Gospels, we see here no simple
progression from one Palestinian Targum to another.
Each is distinctive in some way, and yet at the same
time is related positively to the other three
(collectively, and sometimes individually).
Structurally, the phenomena to be accounted for can be
imagined in a schematic way (cf. the sigla in the
textual presentation and the discussion above):

```
CG:  AI AII
PJ:  AI AII BI BII
 N:  AI AII BI BII
FT:  BI AI BII AII.
```

Basically, a theological debate (A) has been
elaborated with an argument about theodicy (B). The
latter material has influenced the presentation of the

former (in N), even to the extent that it usurps pride of place (in FT). Our scheme is a responsible way in which to understand the lay of the evidence, so long as it is borne in mind that it implies nothing about the substantive priority of one Targum over another (in that CG, for example, might as well be an abbreviation of the others as their starting point), that it does not take account of the linguistic links noted above, which establish a mutual relationship of commonality and distinctiveness among the Targums, and that therefore simple literary dependence cannot be deduced from the susceptibility of the evidence to analysis along structural lines.

The sort of structural relationship described above can be instanced in the passage from the Synoptic Gospels chosen for analysis, i.e., at Matthew 12:22-30; Mark 3:22-27; Luke 11:14-23. After the statement of the charge that Jesus is possessed (v. 22), Mark has Jesus reply. This response, said to be parabolic (v. 23a), presents a simple argument: the claim that Satan casts himself out is ludicrous (vv. 23b-26), since only a power greater than Satan's could do that (v. 27). We may designate this argument as "A," and we must distinguish it from the second line of argument ("B"), presented only by Matthew and Luke. There we find elaborations: if I, Jesus asserts, exorcise by Beelzebul, so do your exorcists (Matthew 12:27/Luke 11:18c-19), and in any case my exorcisms are a sign of the kingdom (Matthew 12:28/Luke 11:20). Additionally, Matthew (12:30) and Luke (11:23) close the entire pericope with the saying, "Who is not with me is against me...." At one level, the procedures followed by Matthew and Luke in presenting their "B" material are identical. Each introduces the new argument after the question, "how will his (Satan's) kingdom stand?" (Matthew 12:26c/Luke 11:18b), where Mark has the simple declaration (3:26c), "he is not able to stand, but has an end." The shift from an assertion to a question is rhetorically effective, since it smooths the entry of the question which opens the new material ("And if I by Beelzebul cast out demons, by whom do your sons cast them out?" [Matthew 12:27a, b; Luke 11:19a, b]). That is, a relative

change is made in "A" material in order to develop its
relationship with "B" material, a technique we saw
illustrated in Pseudo-Jonathan, Neophyti I and the
Fragments Targum. After the kingdom saying (Matthew
12:28; Luke 11:20), Matthew and Luke both return to
the parable of binding the strong man (Matthew 12:29;
Luke 11:21-22), which is also found in Mark (3:27).
Matthew more closely approximates the Markan diction
than does Luke (although even it deviates from Mark),
but it maintains the rhetorical continuity between
"A"and "B" material by introducing the image with
another question beginning with πῶς, and ἤ only serves
to underline this continuity. Luke's diction, on the
other hand, departs markedly from both Matthew's and
Mark's in this section, and yet it is nearer than
Matthew to Mark in the assertive form in which it
presents the parable. We are reminded of the formal
similarity in the context of marked deviation between
the Cairo Geniza fragment and the Fragments Targum.
Luke also deviates substantively from its colleagues
in the addition of 11:16 ("And others, tempters,
demanded a sign from him") which is paralleled
elsewhere in Mark (8:11) and Matthew (16:1).

     The tendency in Matthew and Luke, in contrast to
Mark, is to focus on the christological dimension of
Jesus' debate with his accusers. His exorcisms attest
the kingdom; who is not with him is against him.
Substantive, linguistic adjustments in the material
held in common with Mark sharpen the focus further.
Jesus reads his opponents' minds (Matthew 12:25a; Luke
11:17a, cf. Mark 3:23a), and the kingdom he opposes is
not merely not able to stand (Mark 3:24), but laid
waste (Matthew 12:25b; Luke 11:17b). Such an emphasis
might seem at odds with the saying which immediately
follows the complex in Matthew, which exculpates
blasphemy against the son of the man in its insistence
that blasphemy against the spirit is unforgivable
(Matthew 12:31-32). This tension does not occur in
Luke, where the saying appears in a different context
(12:10); but Matthew is not here following the Markan
tradition precisely (3:28-30), since no mention is
found there of blasphemy against the son of man.

Matthew is therefore closer to Luke in diction, and to Mark in order, and the impact of its presentation is to provide some balance to 12:30 ("Who is not with me is against me ..."). This saying is the reverse of Mark 9:40 ("Who is not against us is for us."). To some extent, Matthew has softened the contradiction by appending 12:31-32 to v. 30. Luke does no such thing, but it presents a parallel to Mark 9:40 (at 9:50b), albeit not in proximity to the Beelzebul controversy, but in a context which accords with Mark's. But the remark in Luke concerns anyone who is against/for "you," so that a christological implication in possible conflict with 11:23 is avoided. A complex, three-handed interrelationship among the Synoptics is evident. We can therefore see among the Gospels the sort of non-linear connections which we discovered among the Palestinian Targums, cognate conflations of tradition resulting in tension between "A" and "B" material, and the attempt to resolve that tension.

In a recent treatment of the redactional procedure of Josephus, F. Gerald Downing remarks ([1980] 33): "It is not the divergences among the synoptists (or even between them and John), in parallel contexts, that are remarkable: it is the extraordinary extent of verbal similarities.... The relationship may betoken a much greater respect, one for the other, even than Josephus' for Scripture." He nonetheless concludes that "The example of Josephus' procedure reinforces the credibility of the four-document hypothesis" (p. 47). Part of his argumentation is that the recent counter-proposal that the documents in question were formed by midrashic procedures fails to offer "any at all precise precedent or analogy for Gospels so conceived" (pp. 46-47). Although the thesis of Goulder, Drury, and their predecessors has not yet been subject to full critical treatment, their resort to an *ex hypothesi* case is evident and -- on Drury's own admission -- can lead to a "certain totalitarianism, with resulting strain" ([1980] 73). The present discussion, however, proceeds from the observation of the sort of "precedent or analogy for Gospels" in their synoptic relations which Downing calls for.

If the Synoptic Gospels are analogous to the Palestinian Targums, what of that? The Gospels are not Targums, not interpretative translations of scripture into Aramaic (or, for that matter, into Greek). Such an analogy, then, can only suggest that the Gospels were transmitted much as the Targums were, as essentially oral compositions ultimately fixed in written form. A defined point of departure is also offered by the Targums for understanding the development of Jewish, oral tradition for the benefit of the faithful, not only the learned, before, during, and after the period in which the New Testament took shape. In the present case, we have observed that procedures analogous to shaping, conflating, restructuring, and theologically synthesizing material in Matthew, Mark, and Luke seem to be operative in the Cairo Geniza fragments, Pseudo-Jonathan, Neophyti I, and the Fragments Targum. The kaleidoscopic relationship among the four Palestinian Targums, in which the evident, often verbatim contact between the Targums is combined with striking individuality, has not proved susceptible of an analysis under which one document fully explains another. The supposition of a literary hierarchy of influence might appear even less convincing in respect of the Synoptic Gospels if we had recourse to as many witnesses to their traditions as we do in the case of the Palestinian Targums. But if there is anything in our proposed analogy, then perhaps it will lead us to dispense with the attempt to establish purely literary priority among our Gospels.

Our model would then be that of a common tradition transmitted in a way which permitted of individual development and of mutual influence at every level in the course of its emergence. The interpretative process of transmission was, later in the day, probably more self-consciously literary than at the beginning (particularly in the case of Luke); this observation applies also to the Targums, in that the scribal and/or recensional activities involved in producing four separate versions did not likely occur in four culturally isolated centers. But such written work was but one stage in a progressive continuum. To try to press all of the development of the Synoptic tradition into this one stage when there are evident analogies in the Targumic tradition, which we can see to be the product of interrelation at more than one level of transmission, is illegitimately to force folk, Jewish literature into the mold of Western literary activity. The objection commonly raised against a form critical-approach to the New Testament -- that it presupposes centuries of development before oral tradition achieved written form -- is not altogether relevant here: the criterion of language puts the recension of the Palestinian Targums within a single epoch in the development of Aramaic, and their substantive reflection of Amoraic theology leads to the same conclusion. They appear to have emerged during this period, in oral or written form, with a basic, exegetical framework in which earlier material was included and on which later views were hung (cf. Marmorstein [1931] 241-242; Chilton [1982]). That is, the period during which they achieved a recognizable form as Targums is more restricted than the period including all of the material they present. This should hardly surprise us, nor is the situation qualitatively different in the case of the Gospels, in which pre-Christian material is evident to any tradition critic, and readings which supplement the work of the originally published forms are obvious to any textual critic.

PART THREE: CONCLUSIONS

ORIENTATION IN THE STUDY OF SYNOPTICITY

Our study of passages evincing synopticity in the New Testament and Rabbinica has made it possible heuristically to develop a vocabulary of comparison. Materially, passages might convey haggadoth with structures and themes that appear mutually relating. That was the case in Study 1, which may be taken as treating of a classic instance of synopticity, as it is usually understood. Both Yoḥanan ben Zakkai and Jesus are identified as the wellsprings of positions which are variously construed in the texts which convey them. "Construal," in fact, is the best description of a text, with reference to those other texts with which it forms a synoptic relationship, when haggadoth are at issue whose structures and themes are congruent. Study 2, however, in its treatment of passages concerning Hillel and Jesus, revealed that comparable material may be incorporated within structurally distinctive presentations, and that -- as distinctively presented -- material under one set of textual circumstances may convey markedly unusual themes as compared to its presentation within synoptically related texts. To describe such alternative developments, "transformation" appears more apt than "construal." Finally, the stories of Simeon ben Yoḥai and Jesus analyzed in Study 3 demonstrated that passages may be comparable, without being relatable synoptically. A commonly theological language may be spoken within two groups of passages (as in Study 3, one set related to Simeon, the other to Jesus), the texts of each group being synoptic construals of a single, underlying act of promulgated meaning. But the acts of meaning concerned are "performances," linguistic achievements of sense without which the two textual complexes could not exist, and which require no postulation of antecedent acts of meaning in order to become explicable. Those performances, of Simeon and Jesus, are only historical in the literary sense that they are antecedent to the textual construals which are extant, and they evince no connection to one another.

As the first three Studies proceeded, it became plain that the material synopticity among the first three Gospels is not necessarily a "Synoptic Problem," as is almost universally supposed in the discipline today. The "Problem" is, to some extent, merely an artifact of widespread ignorance of Rabbinica. But the last generalization is only sustainable to a defined extend: the boundary is reached when one considers the taxic synopticity of the first three Gospels. A desire to explore taxic synopticity in Rabbinica led us to consider Targumic passages in comparison with the Synoptics in Studies 4 and 5. Before taking up the issue of taxic synopticity, we must first, at least experimentally, explore how an analysis of the Gospels along the lines so far developed might be conducted. In order to pursue that exploration, an investigation of Jesus' teaching of the kingdom will be offered, owing to its centrality within Jesus' position in the Synoptic presentation.

The Performance of the Kingdom: Jesus

Speech concerning God's kingdom was well established within the language of early Judaism at the time of Jesus. We can say with some precision that, at least in the circles that handed on the Targumim, the divine kingdom was understood to refer to God's definitive intervention on behalf of his people. The application of the Targums' dynamic construal of the kingdom, as a presupposition of Jesus' preaching, was developed independently -- and almost simultaneously -- by the present writer ("Regnum" 1978, 1979) and Klaus Koch (1979). Precisely that dynamically eschatological concept (conveyed by the Targums), in which God is conceived of as definitively, yet presently, active, has been taken up in France by Jean Carmignac (1979), in Germany by Helmut Merklein (1983), in Switzerland by Odo Camponovo (1984), and by the present writer in a series published jointly in the United States and Britain (*Kingdom* [1984]). The gist of the revised consensus is that the conception of the kingdom applied by Jesus is that of the Judaism of his time.

His innovation lay, not in any philosophical transformation of Judaism, but in his usage of the kingdom within a pressing, public announcement.

Even at this point, care must be taken in assessing the creativity of Jesus. The simple fact of the matter is that, within early Judaism, the language of kingship could be used to describe the position of Israel:

> A king once invited his subjects to a banquet, but he did not specific a time. Those of his subjects who were clever thought, Everything must be set in the king's house. They dropped their normal duties, dressed themselves formally, and sat waiting at the door of the king's house. But some of the subjects were foolish. They said to themselves, It takes time to prepare a feast. They went about their usual, toilsome work. Suddenly, the king summoned his subjects to the feast; the wise appeared properly attired, while the foolish were work-soiled. The king rejoiced to greet the wise, and was vexed with the foolish. He commanded, Let those, who readied themselves for the feast, sit, eat, and drink. But let those, who did not ready themselves, stand and watch.

The parable is found in Talmud (Shabbath 153a), under the name of Yoḥanan ben Zakkai, and has recently been discussed by David Flusser ([1981] 23). Presently, the parable is given a context in which individual repentance (and death) is the issue, but that is secondary to its intrinsically eschatological meaning. Notably, an anonymous parable in Shabbath 152b introduces an ethical theme of similar motifs, in that a king hands out royal garments which he expects to be kept tidy until his return. We who are familiar with the Gospels might feel we have met this whimsical king before. In Matthew 22, for example, the same sort of king throws a feast, in this case a wedding feast, for some palpably unworthy invitees. The first lot fails to show up, despite adequate warning (vv. 3-5), and even kills those sent to fetch them (v. 6), while the second lot includes all manner of riffraff (vv. 8-10). Indeed, the whimsical king himself has one of his guests thrown out for being badly dressed (vv. 11-14), although the hastily invited fellow has scarcely had time to change. The king of Matthew 22 is erratically generous, and vindictive, as is the king in the simpler story with which we began.

Jews in the first century were well acquainted with the deadly whimsy of kings. The Gospels have it that Herod Antipas ordered John the Baptist beheaded in an excess of zeal for his niece's dancing and her mother's choreography (see Matthew 14:3-12; Mark 6:17-29). Whether or not that charge is true (and Josephus' version of the matter must give us pause), the fact remains that the people for whom the story was intended thought Herod capable of acting as he is described. Josephus specifically attributes to Antipas the fear that John's eloquence might lead to some sort of insurrection (cf. L.H. Feldman, [1969] 82, 83, cf. *Antiquities* XVIII.5.2 @ 118).

The royal whimsy in our two parables, then, is not unrealistic, when judged from the point of view of what subjects expected of their rulers in the first century. That feature of both stories appears unmotivated at first sight, but further acquaintance with our texts undermines that impression. Herod Antipas, as presented in Matthew and Mark, is whimsical because he is a vacillating pawn in the hands of his wife and her daughter (his niece). The very marriage John condemned Herod for entering (Matthew 14:3, 4; Mark 6:17, 18) is what turns the fearful ruler (Matthew 14:5; Mark 6:20) into an inflamed murderer. Herod's whimsy finds its motivation in the narrative line of the story of his progressive corruption. What is comparable to that feature in the two stories about kings we have just considered? The short answer to our question would appear to be: nothing.

Matthew's king behaves with surreal generosity in inviting unworthy guests; their refusal to accompany the king's servants at the appointed hour is inexplicable effrontery (v. 5), while their assault on and murder of those servants seems absurdly exaggerated (v. 6). His reaction to their refusal and their crime, in sending troops to kill and and burn their entire city (22:7), is also extreme. That reaction is, or course, quite inappropriate, and is conventionally regarded as a folk motif which has been introduced secondarily, to reflect the burning of Jerusalem in A. D. 70 (cf. Jeremias [1972] 68). Such is probably the case, but the discovery that a narrative feature is secondary does not answer the basic question, What is it doing in the story? The only actual text to be understood is the one before our eyes, not a hypothetically more original version. In the present story, the king's inappropriate response does not serve to discredit him (as in the legend about Herod), but occasions a fresh invitation to others (vv. 8-10). Even among them, of course, not all are found suitable by the king (vv. 11-13, which are also widely regarded as secondary, and so are not infrequently ignored; cf. Jeremias [1972] 65, 66). No explanation of this behavior, positive or negative, is stated (or intimated); that is simply the way the king is.

The king in the first story we encountered is less volatile, but perhaps no more reasonable. No one normally announces a feast without mentioning when it will take place, and to punish people for their productive labor, while commending servants for lying about preening themselves, seems surreal, even by the least capitalistic of standards. (To the extent that the parable in Talmud is preceded by another of a similar theme [Shabbath 152b], this surreal aspect is perhaps somewhat reduced in the received form of the text; what at first sight is surprising is explained by a literary, if not a narrative line, somewhat as in the story of Herod and John the Baptist.) As in the case of Matthew 22, no blame attaches to this royal fecklessness. Such is the king's way. In narrative terms, there is no explanation, praise, or blame: just the stark fact of the king's whimsy. What we are faced with in both stories is a narratively unmotivated, but emphatic, motif. Call it the king's whimsy, or caprice, or sovereign authority, or whatever you will, the surrealism of the motif seems evident. Both stories certainly have realistic elements, but reality is stretched (perhaps to the breaking point in Matthew) where the behavior of the king (and even of his subjects) is concerned.

The strange behavior of subjects is known within the world of Jewish parables, as a story attributed to Rabbi Nathan indicates. The story appears in the Semaḥoth of Rabbi Ḥiyya 3, in the edition of Michael Higger (1931), and it is cited by Flusser ([1981] 24). In the story, a king builds a palace, brings in servants, and entrusts them with gold and silver. Warning them not to steal, he goes to another province. The servants proceed to do precisely what they were told not to do, so that by the time the king returns, he finds them having so exploited one another, they are standing naked outside the palace. After that starkly surreal image, the action of the king -- in taking back the goods -- strikes the reader as the only realistic element in the tale.

Of course, we are not surprised by this aspect of the stories, because we know they are parables. In both cases, the king is permitted his whimsy, because the entire story is a narrative metaphor designed to speak of God. The term "parable" can be used in the ancient sense, of any figurative aphorism or proverb, but modern ears find that usage strange. Is the following statement a parable: "It is not what enters the mouth which defiles one, but what proceeds from the mouth defiles one" (Matthew 15:11)? Matthew 15:15 so identifies it, and that identification accords with the loose definition of "parable" in the first century. But modern usage requires more than a metaphorical or gnomic element to identify a statement as a parable: the metaphor needs to be extended by narrative means, as in the characteristic stories of Jesus. In each of the stories under consideration, the oddity of the king's actions reminds us that we are not dealing with a king of "flesh and blood" (cf. the Rabbinic usage of this phrase, as in Shabbath 152b), but with a narrative metaphor of divine action.

The motif of the king is in each case somewhat surreal; it will not do to ask why, in narrative terms, the kings are whimsical. The mere fact of their whimsy is an aspect of what is conveyed by the parables. But what does that motif do to us as hearers? In a story told entirely within realistic terms, unmotivated actions or characterizations are flaws in the plot: we find ourselves less engaged by what happens as a result of stray events. If any realistically portrayed character is ambivalent, we want an explanation, or at least the chance to understand why that might be. But our two parables function in a different way: their portrayals of the king must be surreal in order to make a divine reference possible.

The divine king, such parables claim, is not what might be expected. And that element of the unanticipated awakens a response in any hearer who takes the parables at their word, as portrayals of God. If, as in the first parable, God is a generous, but punctilious king, his invitation to fellowship must be embraced immediately and patiently, even to the exclusion of ordinary duty. If, as in the second parable, the divine king sends messengers, it is obvious that no ordinary duties should stand in the way of accepting their guidance to the feast; should any be so dim as to refuse that guidance, fresh opportunities are available, but not for those who are unprepared. A demand for readiness, even to the point of challenging the conventional understanding of duty, is addressed by both of the parables. In addition to motifs which portray the king, the parables articulate ethical themes which catch the hearer up in their surreal world. Indeed, only an attendance on the narrative motifs of the parable, understood metaphorically, can convey the ethical theme. For however odd the king may appear by the standards of flesh and blood, such parables claim, he is the actual king of Israel's experience.

The parables we have discussed do not function simply as discourse, or even story; rather, they perform the meaning which is their burden. What it means for God to be king is conveyed by means of narrative metaphor in both instances. There are religious concepts, such as that of the divine kingdom or kingship, which do not lend themselves to being expressed by purely discursive -- or even purely narrative, or purely metaphorical -- means. Notably, the kingdom is never formally defined, or described, in the documents of early Judaism and Christianity. Conceptually, the phrase "kingdom of God" merely refers to the fact, or the claim, that God will intervene on behalf of his people: how, when, and where he rules are disclosed only by particular statements in context. The parables we have considered function by virtue of their very impurity as literary forms: they are effective as performances of the kingdom precisely because they are surprising hybrids, as judged by what a hearer might anticipate.

Within the language of Judaism, and of the movement which came to be known as Christianity, it was perfectly possible to say, "Your kingdom is an everlasting kingdom" (Psalm 145:13), while praying that God's kingdom might soon prevail (as in the Kaddish and the Lord's Prayer; cf. D.W. Staerk [1910] 30, 31; Brocke, Petuchowski, Strolz, [1974] 43, 44). The temporal bugbear, whether the kingdom should be taken as present and/or future, might be considered implicit within this range of usage, but somehow this logical problem (as it has seemed to modern scholarship) was not raised within the sources themselves. The two parables at issue here offer performances of the kingdom, which portray God by means of surreally royal motifs. But how is it they do not settle the question of the time of the kingdom, and fail to show any sign of being disturbed by such a question?

As the parables apply to us, we do not know whether the invitation to feast with the king has been sent, or even whether the feasting has already commenced. We might imagine the parabolic scenes as wholly in the future, entirely past, or as some mixture of past, present, and future. However much we fiddle with the frame of time, neither the surreal motifs nor the ethical themes of the parables are thereby better appreciated. By asking when the parabolic events are posited, we only distance ourselves from the force of stark motifs and of urgent calls for readiness. The only temporal frame which matters, within the logic of what we are told, is the one which runs from the king's resolve to have a feast up to its accomplishment. That tension between promise and fulfillment, the field within which people act, is what matters; to assign them specific times only evades that tension, and so misses the parables' point. If the tension between what the king decides to do, and what finally occurs, is made purely past or purely future, it is obviously only of theoretical interest, and the ethical import of both parables is lost. Even a frame inclusive of both present and future might prove misleading, because the present of one hearer is the past or future of other hearers. Moreover, a hearer might respond to the parabolic imperative in one "present" moment, only to ignore it in another. Both parables function on the understanding that God determines and acts, and that people find or loose themselves in the midst of that dialectic. To seek to know the precise temporal reference of the parables is to chase the wind, and to miss their movement.

Both of the parables we have considered effect performance, as portrayals of God and as encitements to action on the basis of those portrayals. Each may fairly be described as eschatological, or, at any rate, as consistent with eschatology, in that -- whatever stance the hearer takes temporally -- the parabolic movement is towards a full disclosure of God's kingdom in the future. There is evidently a lack, and even a rejection, of temporal precision in this focus on the future, so that the description of these parables as "apocalyptic" appears untenable. But their irreducibly eschatological orientation seems manifest. Precisely that eschatological aspect is what Flusser consistently misses, in his adherence to the construal of Jesus' teaching offered by C. H. Dodd (cf. Flusser [1981] 64, 66, 67; and the discussion in Chilton, J.I.H. McDonald [1987]).

If the first parable appeared within the corpus of Jesus' sayings, few doubts about its authenticity would be expressed. Its motifs and themes are consistent with his teaching generally, and -- at the same time -- the parable is not merely a derivative version of what is stated better elsewhere. Moreover, to describe the performance simply as narrative or story would be misleading, since it concerns more than what it names. There are certainly no signs of that bane of every dominical parables's existence: secondary interpretation in the interests of the Church. Indeed, it would be most peculiar if such signs were evident, because the parable is ascribed, not to Jesus, but to a younger contemporary, the eminent rabbi Yoḥanan ben Zakkai (Shabbath 153a).

At this stage, of course, what seems a merely literary inquiry might -- and has -- become the occasion of Jewish-Christian polemics. The results of that metamorphosis can be appalling. The attempt is commonly made to portray one of the parables as a mere imitation of the other (cf. Jeremias [1972] 12), as if Jesus or Yoḥanan lacked the creativity to tell a decent parable on his own account. In fact, of course, the only similarity between the two stories is in the whimsy of a king who first makes generous provision for a banquet, and then proves to be choosy about the guest list. The plot, structure, and diction of the two stories are so different that no attempt would be made to relate them genetically, apart from the lure of polemic victory.

Even were such a victory possible in this case, it would be Pyrrhic. If Jesus' parable derived from Yoḥanan's, or the reverse, the polemic argument has it that the earlier formulation explains the later so adequately that it need not be considered further. Only what is earliest counts. A similar approach is evident among those critics of the New Testament who seem convinced that any interpretative elements which were incorporated as the documents were composed are, by definition, of no value (or, at least, of lesser account). Such an approach is quite insensitive to the power of persons and texts, of whatever period, to innovate within an accepted system of theological language (or to refer uniquely to an historical reality). Jesus and Yoḥanan, whatever their precise relationship, each expresses a view of God's kingdom on the basis of a common understanding of what the divine rule means. They have not put their signatures to the texts which are presently available, but the similar style of the two passages (coming, as they do, from quite different sources) tends to support the first century provenience of them both. Be that as it may, each articulates a call readily to accept the invitation of a whimsical, and ultimately sovereign, king. In them both, the reality of a coming kingdom demands that a narrative metaphor of celebration and challenge be performed. That performance, of course, is a literary fact of the text to hand, not -- by itself -- a claim of literal historicity. "Jesus" and "Yoḥanan" are for us the names of performed meanings conveyed by certain documents; any speculations concerning those persons can only take place in the form of reasoning abstracted from the cognitive reality of texts.

Because the meaning of the two parables is plain, and all the plainer when they are seen in relationship, the attempt to explain either of them away on the basis of some antecedent is theologically counter-productive. The meaning which is there, inherent in texts, offers itself to be considered, not to be dissolved in a series of hypothetically earlier sources. The chase for the earliest form of an idea, if pursued uncritically, will ultimately dissolve any meaningful statement into a set of constituents which, in themselves, have no meaning. That corrosive technique can be turned as easily on Jesus' sayings as on Yoḥanan's, to the benefit of no one. There is, of course, no gainsaying that a statement ascribed to Yoḥanan in Talmud, or a statement ascribed to Jesus in the Gospels, is likely to have been shaped and colored by those who passed it on. In order to answer certain questions, it is necessary to distinguish layers of interpretation, insofar as that it possible, from more original teaching (cf. Chilton [1979]). But our questions may also center on the texts we have actually received, in this case, on the mutually defining purposes of two parables. In the two that have been considered, we see evidenced the respective performances of Jesus and Yoḥanan, followed by their successors (who handed on their stories orally and scribally). That performance, the honed presentation

of God as king, intends to elicit the performance of
the kingdom by hearers, who are to seek to act in
obedience to the divine whimsy which is conveyed.
Those who hear with the ears of responsive obedience
join with those, nameless predecessors who heard such
stories, and could not keep them to themselves.

Transformations and Construals of the Kingdom

The appropriate focus of research concerning Jesus is
not his alleged "uniqueness," or a "transformation" of
Judaism. Such categories are more homiletic than
anything. Even in that context, the rhetoric is at
best hollow, and it may foment that unreflective
denigration of all things Jewish which is more
pervasive than the existence of overt anti-Semitism
might suggest. In his announcement and parabolic
promulgation of the kingdom, Jesus is distinctive, but
not unique, original, but not exotic. His preaching
and teaching of the kingdom are worked out in the
categories and vehicles of early Judaism, and they
share with such rabbis as Yoḥanan ben Zakkai the
axiomatic faith in God's imminent and kingly rule, his
powerful intervention on behalf of his people.

What is characteristic of Jesus is the
performance of the kingdom which his sayings convey.
To speak of any conceptual shift from the received
language of his day to his own definitions is probably
misleading. It appears helpful, however, to give play
to the sayings ascribed to him as evidencing his
distinctive position, and to speak of further
developments of his perspective. Throughout our
discussion, however, it is vital to recall that we are
discussing the performed meaning of texts, and their
reference to "Jesus" as the antecedent of that
performance. Any immediate transfer of our findings to
"the historical Jesus" would be conceptually premature
(cf. Study 3).

In general terms, one may refer to a
transformation of language of the kingdom, or of any
conceptually rich language, provided there exists a
prior standard of discourse which the transformed

usage palpably takes up. In the case of Jesus, there is no evidence that he transforms some standard sort of talk regarding the kingdom. The appearance is rather that he offers his own characteristic performance of various possibilities of theological language, in a manner comparable to, albeit distinctive from, that of Yoḥanan ben Zakkai. There is too much fluidity within early Judaism in respect of the kingdom to make the claim of "transformation" tenable in respect of Jesus, or of any contemporaneous Jewish teacher. Notably, however, a transformation of "kingdom," as a defined performance, does take place when the corpus of Jesus' sayings is embedded in the narrative framework of Gospels, whose order follows his ministry.

It is arguable that a degree of transformation is inevitably an aspect of traditional transmission. Yoḥanan's parable in Shabbath 153a is preceded by the similar, but unattributed, performance in Shabbath 152b. Whether or not Yoḥanan had anything to do with the first parable, the simple fact is that no sensitive reader can fail to recall it when Yoḥanan speaks in Shabbath 153a. The relationship between the two parables creates a field in which their meaning is conveyed. No matter how "accurately" they have been "passed on," the apparently innovative juxtaposition creates a dimension of meaning which would otherwise not exist. (The language which scholars of the New Testament typically use, in their fixation with the collection of words used in a traditional teaching, sometimes obscures the impact which context has in the reception of any message.) Precisely the same sort of observations obtain, *mutatis mutandis*, in the case of the collection of Jesus' parables in Matthew 13, Mark 4, and Luke 8: in each case, the contextualization is unique, in view of the inclusion, exclusion, and ordering of material.

The power of contextualization is such, that a new language of tradition needs to be framed. If we are fixated at the stage of imagining tradents "passing on" data "accurately" (or not), we fail to understand the process which is under investigation. Neusner has helpfully referred to such a conception as fomenting a distorted impression of tradition as "sedimentary" ([1987] 2, 3]): datum is held to be added to datum in an endless process of accretion, in which one tradition can be directly linked to another, in a document of a totally different period, purpose, and ethos, all in the theoretical name of "intertextuality." Neusner has rightly insisted that tradents do not neutrally transmit data; rather, they say things with reference to predecessors. Their meaning is to be defined systemically, with an eye to the particular documents which tradents actually contributed to. Only such a revised understanding of tradition can possibly do justice to those developments which occasioned the Gospels.

Before we proceed to discuss what is achieved by contextualization in each Synoptic Gospel, however, it is necessary to explain that there is a commonly Synoptic transformation of the kingdom. The transformation is sufficiently general so that the construal of each Synoptic Gospel may be described as variations on a theme, while it is so distinctive that no other ancient document may be described as sharing it. The transformation introduces the kingdom as preached by Jesus (Matthew 4:17, 23; 9:35; 12:28; Mark 1:15; Luke 4:43; 8:1; 9:2; 10:9, 11; 11:20). This obvious feature of the Gospels' narratives is no less influential for being evident: the kingdom from this point onwards is established as the burden of Jesus' message and no other's. Moreover, an acceptance of him involves embracing the characteristic understanding of the kingdom which unfolds.

The next major phase in the Synoptic transformation of the kingdom is pedagogical. The Jesus who is the kingdom's herald is also its advocate, who explains its features to those who hear, and yet are puzzled (or even scandalized). The extent of the material each Gospel devotes to this phase varies greatly, but in every case it is the largest phase (Matthew 5:3, 10, 19, 20; 6:10, 33; 7:21; 8:11,12; 11:12; 13:11, 19, 24, 31, 33, 38, 41, 43, 44, 45, 47, 52; 16:19; 18:1, 3, 4, 23; 19:12, 14, 23; 20:1; 21:31, 43; 22:2; 23:14; 24:14; 25:1, 34; Mark 4:11, 26, 30; 9:1, 47; 10:14, 15, 23, 24, 25; 12:34;

Luke 6:20; 7:28; 8:1, 10; 9:11, 27, 60, 62; 11:2; 12:31; 13:18, 20, 28, 29; 16:16; 17:20, 21; 18:16, 17, 24, 25, 29; 21:31). The distribution of this material varies, but it is striking that none of the Synoptic Gospels invokes the term "kingdom" as a link to include all statements on the subject in a single complex of material. Such an association by catchword is indeed detectable over short runs of material, so that isolated sayings are the exception, not the rule, but in no case is subject matter or wording the solely determinative influence on context. Rather, there is a narrative contextualization, in which Jesus' activity in preaching, teaching, and disputing becomes the governing framework for a given run of sayings (cf. Chilton [1979] 11-23, for a categorization of Jesus' sayings). Those frameworks vary from Gospel to Gospel, of course, as do the logia presented; the distribution of sayings can certainly not be explained by reference to some fixed, historical ordering. The point is rather that the typically Synoptic transformation of Jesus' preaching embeds the kingdom within his ministry, so that he and the kingdom approximate to being interchangeable. The particular textual moves that achieve this identification vary: the fact that it is achieved does not.

The last phase of the Synoptic transformation of the kingdom pursues the logic of the identification: Jesus' death and the kingdom are presented as mutually explicating. "I shall not drink of the fruit of the vine again, until I drink it with you new in God's kingdom" (cf. Matthew 26:29/Mark 14:25/Luke 22:18). Whatever the sense of that saying was within the ministry of Jesus, within the Synoptics it serves to insist that the same Jesus who announced and taught the kingdom is also the sole guarantor of its glorious coming (cf. the similar function of Luke 22:29, 30; 23:42). The notices in Mark (15:43) and Luke (23:51) -- that Joseph of Arimathea was one of those who anticipated the kingdom -- serve to underscore just this feature of the Synoptic transformation.

The Synoptic transformation of the kingdom essentially involves a unique pattern of the distribution of sayings, and of their narrative contextualization within Jesus' ministry. The result is to focus upon Jesus as the herald, advocate, and guarantor of the kingdom in an innovative fashion. Arguably, the transformation explicates what is implicit within the sayings' tradition: an awareness that Jesus' ministry is a seal of the kingdom. The most obvious instance of such a claim within his sayings is Jesus' observation concerning his exorcisms and the kingdom (Matthew 12:28; Luke 11:20). But such implications are no more than that, and observing them only heightens by contrast the Synoptic transformation, in which Jesus' preaching of the kingdom becomes the seal of his divine mission, not the principal point at issue. He who witnessed the kingdom is, within the Synoptics, attested as God's son by virtue of his own message. Precisely because a signal adjustment of precedence between Jesus and the kingdom has taken place, the language of "transformation" is appropriate.

In view of its distinctiveness from the sense of the kingdom in other documents of early Judaism and Christianity, the Synoptic transformation is a particular framing of Jesus' sayings, not merely a loose characterization of similar material in three Gospels. How the transformation was effected, whether by literary borrowing from one document to another, or the sharing of a now lost antecedent, is a matter of conjecture. The history of such speculation is impressively given objective standing by referring to it as "the Synoptic Problem," as if it were a phenomenon of texts, rather than a disturbance among interpreters. The present purpose is not to solve the "Problem," if indeed it is soluble.

The present purpose is rather to profit from the common transformation of the kingdom in the Synoptics in order to describe their particular construals of a single, transformed category (Jesus' preaching). A comparative study of each passage of each Gospel is out of the question, but we can sample the uniquely Matthean, Markan, and Lukan construals of the kingdom.

Within its principal collection of parables, Matthew's Gospel uniquely presents the parable of the man who sows wheat, only to have his field corrupted by an enemy with weeds (13:24-30). In imagery which essentially requires no explanation, the man prudently refuses a suggestion of rooting up the weeds, and leaves that task for the harvest. A more straightforwardly eschatological theodicy would be difficult to contrive. Nonetheless, Matthew offers -- or has Jesus offer -- an explanation of the parable (vv. 36-43). The delay in presenting the explanatory material is notable, in that it results in the framing of the parables of the mustard seed and the leaven (vv. 31-33), as well as a scriptural citation related to the use of parables generally (vv. 34, 35). The wheat and the weeds become governing terms of reference, then, within a complex of material. That entire complex gives an unusual twist to the parable of the sower and its interpretation (vv. 1-23), which (in accordance with the Synoptic transformation as a whole) precedes immediately. The explanation given to the story of the wheat and the weeds heightens the eschatological impact of the parable, by its reference to the son of man, the κόσμος, the devil, the end of the age, angels, the furnace of fire, and the just shining as the sun. Both the imagery itself, and the method of providing a story with a (somewhat redundant) explanation are typical of apocalyptic literature.

The Matthean Jesus gives his explanation to his disciples, with whom he is alone in a house, having left the crowds (v. 36a). The disciples hear three further parables (vv. 44-50), and are then asked by Jesus whether they understand all they have been told (v. 51a). Their affirmative answer introduces the reply that every scribe "discipled" (μαθητευθείς) for the kingdom is as a householder who can produce new and old from his treasure. An apocalyptic interpretation of the kingdom and of Jesus' parables is therefore recommended as the path of scribal discipleship.

Within the Synoptic transformation of the kingdom, there is no doubt but that discipleship is, pre-eminently, the occasion on which Jesus' message might be realized. The mystery of the kingdom belongs to them or to nobody (cf. Matthew 13:11; Mark 4:11;

Luke 8:9). As we have already seen, however, the
Matthean construal particularly heightens the
apocalyptic consciousness which is entailed in
following Jesus. Mark also presents a unique parable
of growth (4:26-29), in a position analogous to
Matthew's story of wheat and weeds. The unique parable
is commonly called "the seed growing secretly," and
Jeremias proposes a different designation, "the
patient husbandman" ([1972] 151, 152). Both
designations are notable for what they conceal about
the parable. The seed grows neither secretly, nor by
itself. A man casts the seed, sleeps and wakes, while
the seed grows. The earth bears fruit as of itself,
until harvest. The co-operative activity conveyed by
the parable is certainly not attested by focusing on
the seed alone. By the same token, Jeremias's
reference to the patience of the husbandman is
approximately as mysterious as the reference in James
5:11 to the patience of Job. When the parable has the
man sleep and wake, the purpose is not to commend his
Stoic accord with the dictates of duty and reason, but
to emphasize that he is wholly ignorant where it
concerns the actual growth of the seed. The image of
the man is superseded by that of the earth. Just at
that point, when the narrative adjustment of metaphor
seems to have been resolved in the image of harvest,
the man appears again. Jeremias stresses the
purposeful activity of the man, and on that basis
attributes patience to him, and identifies him with
Jesus. Indeed, Jeremias treats this parable -- as he
does many others -- as an *apologia* of Jesus for his
ministry, in this case in opposition to a Zealot call
to arms. The fact is, however, that the man is not
credited with patience in the parable; his only named
"virtues" are ignorance (of how the seed grows) and
timeliness (in respect of harvest). The ordering of
this parable within the Markan context, after sayings
which concern the rewards of discipleship (cf.
particularly 4:24, 25) makes it seem highly artificial
to take the man as an image of Jesus. Insofar as the
metaphor needs to be deciphered, the semi-conscious
participation of the man, as sower, spectator, and
harvester, accords more with the portrait of the

disciples in Mark than with the profile of Jesus. Participation in and readiness for the kingdom as an experience cognate with that of daily life is conveyed by means of the particular, narrative metaphor and the precise contextualization of this parable.

That the kingdom is is "within you" or "in your midst" is probably the most cherished thought concerning the kingdom in Western Christianity, and yet the thought occurs only in Luke among the canonical Gospels (17:20, 21). The manner of the saying's presentation also gives it a distinctive sense. It appears in a context within Jesus' extensive journey to Jerusalem (9:51-19:27), as described by Joseph Fitzmyer, "From the Third Mention of Jerusalem to the End of the Lucan Travel Account (Luke 17:11-18:14)" ([1981] 138-140). The particular section is comprised of uniquely Lukan materials and/or Synoptic materials which Matthew and Mark place quite differently. Afterwards, what Fitzmyer describes as "The Synoptic Travel Account" is resumed in Luke from 18:15. There can be little doubt, then, but that the presentation as well as the material of Luke 17:20, 21 is distinctly redolent of the Lukan construal of the kingdom.

The peculiarly Lukan complex, 17:11-18:14, presents the saying concerning the kingdom immediately after the story of the Samaritan leper's gratitude (17:11-19), a placement which highlights the ineptitude of "the Pharisees." They must pose questions of a useless nature, while even a Samaritan outcast (vv. 17, 19) knows what must be done. The statement that the kingdom is "within your midst" (ἐντὸς ἡμῶν) is followed by Jesus' statement (to his disciples) that "the days of the son of man" are numbered (v. 22), and what amounts to a foretaste of the Synoptic apocalypse follows (vv. 23-35). To an extent, this complex of material conveys the Lukan concern with eschatology. The entire run is closed off by the parable of the importunate widow, which is eschatologically pointed (cf. 18:1, 9), and by the parable of the Pharisee and the tax collector. (If the latter has any logical connection within the Lukan context [aside from the characteristic antipathy to

"Pharisees"], it may be with what follows, the blessing of the children.) The end is presented as determinative of present experience (ἐντὸς ἡμῶν), and yet as temporally unchartable. The dialectic of the near and far kingdom is consistently found in Luke and Acts (cf. Mattill [1979]). But the primary achievement of the Lukan presentation is the practical equation of the kingdom and christology, as effected (and evidenced) by the ease of transition from the statement about the kingdom in 17:20, 21 to the statement about the son of man in v. 22. The same identification is conveyed (in the reverse order) at the beginning of the ministry in Luke, when Jesus reads Isaiah 61 in a synagogue (4:16-21), and refers to that as preaching the kingdom (4:43). That 17:20, 21 refers, within the Lukan design, to Jesus' presence among the Pharisee, appears a straightforward conclusion.

Obviously, however, the saying might be taken up in a different way, which is precisely what happens in the Gospel according to Thomas:

If those who lead you say to you,
See, the kingdom is in the heaven,
    then the birds of heaven will precede you.
If they say to you,
It is in the sea,
    then the fish will precede you.
But the kingdom is within you and without you.

Contextually, the meaning of *logion* 3 is clear; the first two sayings promise eternal life to the one who seeks and finds the interpretation of Jesus' words, and the present *logion* serves to explain the mystery of the kingdom. This essentially gnostic quest for salvation becomes explicit in the latter half of the *logion*:

When you know yourselves, then you will be known; and you will know that your are sons of the living Father. But if you do not know yourselves, then you are in poverty, and you are poverty.

The latter half of *1*. 3b serves an explanatory purpose in respect of the at first glance cryptic statement that the kingdom is "within you and without you." The inner aspect of the kingdom is knowledge of oneself, which brings one to the point of being known, while the divine transcendence of the kingdom ("without you") guarantees that any failure to know its self-realization is to be left without God, powerless. The kingdom is within one's human capacities, but not under any person's control.

The radical difference between Thomas and Luke, precisely over a saying which both present, underlines Thomas' distinction, not only from the Synoptic Gospels severally, but from the Synoptic transformation generally. Although the extent of similarity of Thomas to the Synoptics is striking at the level of content, the discursive structure of the document gives it a distinctive form. The ministry of Jesus is no longer the focus; the focus is rather the teaching of Jesus, as ordered into a series of responses to interlocutors. The interlocutions concern right leadership (*1*. 12), the end of discipleship (*1*. 18), the place of Jesus (*1*. 24), the promised rest (*1*. 51), the relation between master and disciple (*1*. 61b), the way of discipleship (*1*. 99), the time of the kingdom (*1*. 113). It may be noticed that the kingdom frames the interlocutory pattern, in that it is introduced in *1*. 3 as the leading edge of the sense of Jesus' "secret words," which the interlocutory superscription presents, and closes the pattern of Thomaean topics in *1*. 113; moreover, the kingdom appears more frequently in Thomas than in any other document of early Christianity (cf. Chilton, "The Gospel according to Thomas" [1984]). The kingdom, as a relationship with God which is produced by saving knowledge, is now the center of interest, in a transformation of a new and startling variety.

The substantial difference in transformations, as between the Synoptics and Thomas, brings us to another, distinctive transformation. The Gospel according to John effects a radical reduction in focus on the kingdom: only one statement, about seeing (3:3) or entering (3:5) the kingdom, is ever made. Such explanation as is offered explicates the requirement for this experience, being born "from above" (ἄνωθεν) or "from water and spirit." (The sense of ἄνωθεν, as "from above," rather than "again," seems the preferred Johannine meaning, since Nicodemus is presented in v. 4 as a paradigm of how to misconstrue Jesus' teaching.) The assumption apparently is that no explanation of the kingdom is required. The distinctively Johannine transformation of traditions concerning Jesus does not center on the kingdom, and that is a mark of its singularity. The focus now is on receiving Jesus in such a manner as one might become a child of God (1:12): the Gospel is so consumed with the discursive and narrative issue of attaining eternal life (cf. 3:16) that the kingdom, the vision of what is actually achieved at the point where the eternal meets the temporal, has slipped from view. It is present as the shadow of an undiscussed axiom.

Preliminary Orientation

Our essentially comparative reading of texts has made it possible for us to describe Jesus' preaching of the kingdom as performance, and to distinguish three documentary transformations of that performance: the variegated Synoptic construals (centering respectively on apocalyptic trust, discipleship, and christology), the discursive transformation of Thomas, and the Johannine transition to the issue of eternal life.

To refer to our reading merely as comparative, however, is to evade a central concern. At each level of performance or transformation, one is, of course, constrained by the usual recognition of redactional or traditional patterns, be they dictional, stylistic, or thematic. Much that has been observed here may easily by collated with redaction-critical studies, in particular. Nonetheless, nothing we have seen justifies the conclusion that we have come to know "the redactor" any better than we did before. Our evidence is simply of textual transformations, and sometimes of construals of those transformations, not -- in the first instance -- of the specific contribution of any person or persons within the process. The process is what presents itself for reading, not the anonymous people behind the process. The propriety of a language of "transformation" suggests that the conventional picture, of transmitters of Jesus' position whose quirks need to be learned and compensated for, is in need of drastic revision. The act of handing on tradition, however conservative in its mechanics, substantially transformed Jesus' performance of the kingdom. To personify that complex process as "the Evangelist," or to identify that personification with one level of the process, be it traditional or redactional, is to think more mythologically than critically.

That awareness, however, brings us to the question, whether it is meaningful to speak of "Jesus' performance" at all. In that his position can only be known by means of documentary transformations, can he be spoken of? Just as in the observation of transformations by means of redaction-critical and tradition-critical techniques, so the isolation of Jesus' performance owes a great deal to usual, historical approaches: one places a person in the appropriate context, in this case early Judaism, and then looks for clues that point to the workings of a distinctive human consciousness.

The Jesus of literary history is nothing other than what needs to be posited, given the evidence available, to explain the texts of early Christianity. The various "criteria of authenticity" are simply ways of expressing how that common-sensical approach works out in the case of the material to hand (cf. Stein [1980]). Both the strength and the weakness of the "criteria" is that they present gauges of how traditions about Jesus developed, not of historical accuracy at any given stage in that development. The strength of articulating such criteria is that they might prepare the reader to approach our texts as transformations and construals of performances, as developing vehicles of meaning, rather than as historical chronicles with the odd accretion of theology. But the misimpression might also be formed, that the criteria represent the fixed mechanics of

Synoptic development; the result of any approach of that sort is to homogenize our texts into an undifferentiated process. The evidence of our inquiry, for what it is worth, suggests that variegation must be allowed for, and that the complex interplay of tradition and contextualization was consciously observed in early Judaism and Christianity. But precisely because our tradents raised performance, transformation, and construal to an art form, it is nothing other than a mistake in categories directly to equate the Jesus of literary history with "the historical Jesus." In that the "criteria of authenticity" indulge that confusion, they are bankrupt.

Of course, the materials for synthesizing "the historical Jesus" are largely provided by "the Jesus of literary history." But we cannot, at the end of the present inquiry, pretend that there is a single, unequivocal Jesus of literary history. That figure, called "Jesus" by our texts, is not to be understood in the first instance as an historical personage with a stable character: we are dealing rather with the consciousness implied by a given performance as conveyed by a specific transformation and/or construal. In that there are a multiplicity of documents, "the Jesus of literary history" must reflect the diverse sources of which that Jesus is (no more than) the necessary antecedent. In other words, the literarily historical Jesus is inferred within our cognition of documents; "the historical Jesus" is a further inference, drawn from the literarily historical Jesuses of all the relevant literature and of such other information as might be gleaned.

Philosophically, one might find it necessary to suppose that some specific, historical Jesus lies behind the literary performances, transformations and construals which refer to him. But it is also possible to speculate that certain literary features, and even the substance of the literature, are functions of imagination rather than of reality. The agony between literalist and symbolist readings of scripture has not notably abated since its onset during the Enlightenment, but there is no reason it should be perpetuated in each and every act of reading. Within the present act of reading, we have been encouraged, by our comparative approach to Rabbinica and the Synoptics, to focus upon the immediately cognitive challenge of synopticity. That challenge -- here met with our heuristic development of the meaning of "performance," "transformation," and "construal" -- is to discover the terms of reference within which the congruence and variation of related texts might be appreciated. Our comparative approach has uncovered certain analogies within the literature concerning Hillel, Yoḥanan ben Zakkai, and Simeon ben Yoḥai. Those analogies, in turn, have made it appear that the linkages of specific haggadoth to named rabbis is both problematic and persistent. That is, contradictory or competing assertions are made in respect of a given rabbi, so that historical plausibility is strained, but only that rabbi's name is the literary category of the assertions.

Our response to the philosophical dilemma posed by synopticity is to ignore it. We have done so because that dilemma is generated by an inquiry into an abstraction from an abstraction, the historical Jesus from the Jesus(es) of literary history. The focus of the present inquiry has rather been upon the question, How does meaning unfold within synoptic relationships of texts? Our response has been that performances are both transformed and construed. We have, for the sake of clarity and coherence, permitted ourselves the single abstraction, representing one level of inference from cognition, that a certain consciousness lies at the base of a literary performance (and, subsequently, within any transformation and/or construal) and that such a consciousness is best named after its literary ascription, be it Hillel, Yoḥanan, Simeon, or Jesus, but without prejudice to our adjudication of history. Human consciousness, we have inferred, is involved in the generation of meaning.

A sensitivity to the consciousness which informs texts, and which those texts now elicit in the reader, lies at the heart of the present approach. Quite evidently, the consciousness at issue is of a

religious nature, and centers on "Jesus" in one way or
another. The documents we read present themselves as
reliable representations of him, so that the
historical process which began with him and ended with
those texts is part and parcel of what is to be
understood. (That is precisely what literary history
involves, although -- once again -- it must not be
confused with history as occurrence.) There can be no
wishing away that process by appeal to the literary
search for a single author, be he actual or "implied,"
redactor or "Evangelist." These documents are
composite not only in the sense that they evolved as
the outcome of a considerable process, but also
because they represent themselves as multi-layered
products of conscious faith, whose orientation is to
be found in what went on before.

Insofar as multi-layered composition is an
aspect of that consciousness which the texts elicit,
and which produced them, it is highly superficial to
speak of the simple engagement of their "horizon" with
ours, or of single literary "themes" being their
entire burden. The former program of
oversimplification is evident in the approach of A. C.
Thiselton (1980). Thiselton's very title (*The Two
Horizons*) betrays the tendency of his book: to
simplify Gadamer's understanding of
Horizontverschmelzung in reading scripture, to the
point that two horizons, the text's and the reader's,
are held to be fused. The translation of *Verschmelzung*
as "fusion" (p. 16) is suspect, especially since
Thiselton proceeds, in practice, to argue that readers
should give up their "horizons" to that of scripture.
In any case, to speak of only two horizons in any act
of human understanding (not to speak of reading
multi-layered compositions) is fundamentally naïve.
Precisely the same oversimplification of Gadamer is to
be found in David J.A. Clines, *The Theme of the
Pentateuch* (1978 p. 102), whose book well represents
the use of literary jargon to avoid critical
difficulties in the reading of texts. In the end, both
Thiselton and Clines would sacrifice the reader's
cognition, and all the ambiguities that cognition
implies, to the supposedly univocal "horizon" or

"theme" of the texts at hand. Whether they would take such an uncritical approach to any work to be found outside the canon, is a question they do not address.

The texts at hand point beyond themselves, to the consciousness which produced them; that elementary point appears to be lost on those who would speak of texts in a hypostatic manner, as if they needed to be accepted or rejected merely in their own terms. If a text engages in a language game we might play, too (cf. Thiselton), or if it can be reduced to a truism, such as God fulfills promises (cf. Clines), it can be protected from contradiction, but at the price that it says nothing. So, for example, Thiselton uses Wittgenstein to argue that Paul and James do not contradict one another on the question of faith and works, but that "each has a rich positive view of the grammar of faith, which emerges in the context of a given language-game or language-situation" (p. 427). Thiselton asserts that the alternative to this sort of special pleading would be to ask after faith "*in the abstract*" (p. 427), which on his view is illegitimate. That alternative is misconstrued: the issue in Wittgensteinian terms is how Paul and James are related (given all their similarities and differences) within the language of early Christianity. In that Thiselton fails to address that issue, he protects Christian scriptures from the charge of contradiction, at the cost of any reasonable claim that they are speaking of the same faith. With less sophistication, Clines blandly argues that his thematic Pentateuch functions as story, and as such "functions as reality from beginning to end" (p. 104). Enthused by the inerrancy of story, he proceeds:

> No awkward historical questions about the material of the Pentateuch stand in the way of its efficacy in creating a "world" or in drawing its readers into participation in that world.

That statement is a classic instance of using a modern category ("story") to homogenize the multi-layered composition of scripture. But the fallacy comports well with Clines's attempt to urge, without argument, that scriptures be taken as a privileged horizon. In both Clines and Thiselton, albeit by differing routes, the position attained is that scriptures tell us what to think, provided they can be found in the canon of Protestantism. It is, perhaps, no accident that horizons and literary themes have been emphasized by scholars, and historical investigation played down, just has fundamentalism has become endemic. We certainly give less offense when we abstract scriptures from reality, but we at the same time betray their intended function, as statements about a God who rules actual experience, and we may possibly betray the human integrity of those readers who look to us for guidance in the process of deciding whether and how scriptural claims might be true.

All of this is to say that the historicity of our texts is irreducibly an aspect of what they convey. But it is not the whole of what they convey, as a positivistic historiography would have it. If complaints about "the historical critical method" have any value which compensates for their apparent encouragement of fundamentalism, it is that they rightly insist that no text is adequately explained by a genetic analysis of its parts. Because a text is irreducibly an artifact of human consciousness which verbally incites the reader to consciousness, to make it appear as an epiphenomenon of "empirical" forces and events betrays both text and reader. Reading is the quest to be conscious, not be be explained away. For that reason, we would characterize the Synoptic Gospels as the performances, transformations, and construals of that literarily historical figure they call Jesus, and we infer that religious consciousness is involved with the figure so named.

By one's nature as a reader, texts push and pull at the mind, and the task of exegesis rightly focuses on a phenomenological description of what in a text brings one to a given understanding. There quickly comes a point, however, at which the text as an object of consideration disappears, and is replaced by the text as a seeming subject, an apparent medium of consciousness in dialogue with that of the reader. A consideration of that shift is far beyond the present purpose, but it is -- in principle -- no more (or less) mysterious than that adjustment by which a person becomes cognizant of any consciousness other than his own or her own.

Of course, there is no guarantee, in any dialogue we enter, that we will respect an interlocutor as much at the end of the conversation as at the beginning. The consciousness we discover might seem to us profound, or boring, or addressed to inappropriate concerns, or too deep for us, etc. An openness to the phenomenology of consciousness, both as elicited and represented by texts, cannot guarantee those texts anything like "authority" in advance. Chiefly in respect of the evaluation of authority, the present approach differs from that of Brevard Childs (1985). In that Childs does justice to the coherence of historical and theological readings, his contribution is a signal advance over the fideism represented by Thiselton and Clines. He can say, for example, where they cannot:

> The pre-history of the Fourth Gospel stands in an indirect, dialectic relation to its final form and aids to the extent in which it illuminates the canonical intentionality (p. 38).

The phrase "canonical intentionality," however, represents the seed of my difficulty with Childs. He holds that "canon" may be used to refer to a collection of writings, to the process which organized the writings, and to "the interpretive activity of the modern Christian reader who seeks not only to identify with the received tradition but also truthfully to appropriate the message and to be a faithful recipient of the gospel for the present age" (p. 41). The definition amalgamates three elements which are evidently distinctive: the meaning of texts, as texts; the meaning of texts within the literature of early Christianity; the meaning of texts, and of that literature, to readers today. I would regard the interpretative (as distinct from the systematic) task as complete when textual meanings have been elucidated within the context of documents which are demonstrably

related (as in instances of synopticity): attempts at
wider synthesis in this case will likely only result
in a lack of clarity.

The performance of Jesus, and the
transformations of the Gospels, will no doubt evoke a
wider range of response, and of apathy, than any of us
can guess at. But one thing we might recognize
commonly is that, in his performance of the kingdom,
Jesus set in motion a dynamic of transformation and
construal such that an account of the religious import
of the pertinent texts must be included in any
adequate apprehension of them.

Prospective Orientation

The analysis of the Synoptic Gospels by means of the
language here evolved to describe documents of early
(and rabbinic) Judaism and their materials
comparatively has not "solved" the "Synoptic Problem."
Indeed, at the level of material synopticity, the
suggestion arises that there is no problem to be
solved: the texts of early Judaism simply group
themselves in such relations, owing to their manner of
composition. Neusner has described the dynamic behind
Sotah in Babli, not as an "author," but as an
"authorship" ([1987] 177-205); we, similarly, have
argued that "the Evangelist" is not a single person
(and by no means "the redactor"), but the process
leading from Jesus' performance to particular
construals of given transformations. Once the myth of
"the author" is removed, the context in which material
synopticity is a natural relationship among documents
becomes plain.

The ease with which scholars over the past
hundred years have referred to "the author" of a given
Gospel, as if the personification of the process were
an established fact, is startling. The blithe
assumption also lies at the heart of the theory of
Markan priority. Writing in 1911, William Sanday (as
we have seen) portrayed the authors as scribes, who
read a "paragraph," and then copied from memory, and
in that way produced deviations among the Synoptics,

which are, he admitted, immediately suggestive of the influence of oral tradition (pp. 8-18). Sanday and his colleagues, of course, took within their terms of reference the elements of Markan priority, which Holtzmann had set out in his work of 1863, but it remains surprising that (a) they did not analyze the portrait of the author as a highly individual, literate scribe, (b) that they failed to inquire whether their portrait of the author was probable sociologically (or, as they would more simply have said, historically), (c) that they did not ask whether transcription paragraph by paragraph would account for the textual data to hand, and (d) that they manifested an ignorance of Rabbinica.

The four surprising weaknesses enumerated above are, of course, fatal. Sanday's picture suited a man of leisure with a publisher, resources, and freedom of conscience, much better than it did anyone operating within, or in the penumbra of, early Judaism. His quaint, but vigorously honest, picture of a transcription paragraph by paragraph does no justice to the restructuring, intercalating, and insertion of new material, with which any student of the Synoptics is familiar. Finally, to accept Sanday's picture involves the question, whether one must -- in order to preserve intellectual consistency -- actually look at Rabbinica in an analogous way.

Of course, the last objection can be met, at least in practice, if Rabbinica are regarded as irrelevant. Working within, and later on the basis of, Sanday's seminar, Streeter developed his "Four Document Hypothesis," which involved gifted, imaginative individuals collating identifiable sources; no alternative to the paradigm of an individual author is discussed ([1924] 223-270). In the main, it has not been questioned since. Form criticism, which might have guided the discipline to a more sensible understanding of processive authorship, instead only fed the myth of the Evangelist/redactor, who was now a master of collage: arrangements were held to be more meaningful theologically than isolated "units" of tradition. Pericopae provided data, while context provided significance, in that sterile consensus of mechanically invoked criticisms of "tradition" and "redaction" which evolved after the last war. Most recently, approaches to the Gospels which style themselves as literary earnestly recommend that great strides will be made, if only we approach the "final" work of "the author." Uncertainty in respect of the reality of such a figure only results in "the implied author" being invoked. Come what may, scholars of the twentieth century will see only their own literary reflections at the wellspring of the Gospels.

What is most disturbing about our solipsism is its intransigence. Challenges from Boman (1967), Gerhardsson (1961), Rist (1979) , and now Reicke (1982), are dismissed out of hand, although on the whole, it must be admitted that these contributors court their own dismissal. Arguing that the nature of the Synoptic tradition was "oral," they then fall into the fallacy of authorship themselves, by attempting to identify the sources of such tradition precisely with individual, historical tradents. Advocates of an oral approach have had a fatal weakness for solving "the Synoptic Problem" at the same time as they commend the Gospels as literally apostolic, historically reliable, and spiritually authoritative. Nonetheless, work from this quarter has been far less egregious in its essentially bourgeois assumption of individual authorship than the contributions of Farmer (1976) and Goulder (1978), who simply intensify the image of "the Evangelists" as writers in the modern mode of the middle class. It would be difficult to guess on the basis of most discussion during this century that, prior to the work of Sanday's seminar, the oral approach was dominant in English-speaking scholarship.

B.F. Westcott of Cambridge, while a master at Harrow, wrote his *Introduction to the Study of the Gospels* prior to his return to a chair, and his subsequent enthronement at Durham. Among other things, Westcott argued -- as we have seen -- that the similarities and deviations among the Gospels suggest their dependence on an oral, apostolic Gospel, which set the pattern of publication ([1896] 174-253). John's Gospel was held deliberately to have

established a different pattern, of theological
argument, rather than of proclamation (cf. [1890]
xlif.). Westcott laid relatively little stress on the
identification of the apostolic Gospel with particular
figures in history; in that regard, his investigation
of an oral solution of "the Synoptic Problem" is less
historicist than more recent attempts. Westcott was
concerned to relate the shape of the Gospels,
individually and collectively, to their function
within the Church, not merely to the intentions of the
people who may (or may not) have composed them.

Conceptually, Westcott's approach was more open
than Sanday's to an analysis of the Gospels within the
context of early Judaism, although he did not
undertake such an analysis himself. It has therefore
proved an unfortunate impediment to progress in
research, that neither Sanday, nor any of his
colleagues, even attempted to refute Westcott's
position. The mutual disregard which sometimes
characterizes the relationship between scholars of
Cambridge and Oxford on this occasion has exacted a
price from the discipline of theology. The seminar in
Oxford compounded its insularity by ignoring the work
of V. H. Stanton, whose careful, exegetical work at
Cambridge embedded the Gospels and Jesus within a
sound appreciation of early Judaic sources (1886).
When the most famous participant in Sanday's seminar,
B. H. Streeter, later published *The Four Gospels*
(1924), it proved to be brilliant in its textual
criticism (largely because he refined the principles
and procedures of Westcott and Hort [1901]), but
notable for its lack of consideration that the very
sources which Streeter granted were partially oral may
have been predominantly so. That Judaic documents were
ignored (except Jeremiah, which is compared to "Q"!),
goes without saying.

That we should, only at this late stage, speak
of a change in our orientation towards synopticity as
merely prospective, is hardly to our credit as a
discipline. For generations, Streeter's hypothesis has
been treated as axiomatic, and among the alternatives
to it, only some variant or another of Griesbach's
hypothesis has been considered seriously (cf. Farmer

[1976]). The practically programmatic avoidance of the literature of early Judaism has blinded us in two regards. First, scholars of the New Testament routinely display no awareness of the theological language employed within the Gospels which is redolent of early Judaism: references to Rabbinica are today all too likely to take the form of negative examples of the sort of "Pharisaism" Jesus is alleged to transcend (cf. Riches [1980]). Second, the discipline has an apparently systemic attitude towards documents, represented in its many methods, which can only be described as bourgeois: the facile equation of a literary approach to the Gospels (source-critical, redaction-critical, or rhetorical) with the "mind" of an individual author, takes the breath away. Such an equation is not only intellectually insipid, it advertises itself as simply and utterly bankrupt before any composite, collective corpus. Since the Gospels and Rabbinica are representative of just such literature, it seems obvious that only a radical change in our orientation towards synopticity can remedy our confusion. The issue now is not progress in research, but the choice between options, one difficult, and the other useless.

The first option involves the encounter with primary texts, both of the Gospels and of Rabbinica, and the evolution of a comparative vocabulary, as has been attempted here in a preliminary fashion: until a language of such criticism has emerged, the first option will require competence at first hand in the literatures which are compared. The alternative option, by contrast, offers the security of a vast secondary literature, and the great reservoir of theological generalizations which are founded upon that literature: its drawback is that it describes the work of authors who never existed, and ignores the terms of reference and cultural circumstances in which the Gospels were produced.

A new, critical orientation would take the material synopticity of the Gospels as an index of their character, not a problem to be solved. Scholars educated in how the documents of early Judaism emerged, would attune themselves to distinctive performances, transformations, and construals, and eschew the cheap rhetoric of Jesus' "transcendence" of Judaism. They would describe the emergent meaning without personifying it, and be sensitive to literarily historical reflections of Jesus and others in his movement (both contemporaries and successors). They would leave for another day the question whether the Gospels as literarily historical may be described as literally historical. They would appreciate the Gospels as religious, rather than intentionally historical, discourse, and discover the individuality of documents within the web of their mutual relations, and their comparability with Rabbinica.

Scholars of the new orientation would think of tradition more critically than has been fashionable. They would not imagine pearls on a string, or bricks in a wall, but understand that tradents are people who transform or construe what lies before them. Nobody can "transmit" a saying or story: what is said immediately occupies a fresh context, so that precedent is only one coordinate -- stretching from speaker to source -- in the act of speaking traditionally. The other coordinate is defined by the axis which stretches between speaker and audience. Until the systemic link between what went on before and what a tradent does with his audience is comprehended, all our talk of tradition is misleading. Unless and until our approach is systemic in that sense, we shall continue to be faced with the opposing programs of breaking texts down into their alleged parts, until they disappear, or feeding them into our grandiose biographies of individual, heroic "authors." Either way, we shall wish our texts away, until we learn to appreciate their contexts within early Judaism.

Scholars of the new orientation would cease imagining anything is said by distinguishing between "written" and "oral" tradition. They would appreciate that, within early Judaism, tannaim were held to standards of accuracy which approximate to what we demand of ourselves in writing, and that scribes could be encouraged to engage in creative explication in what we have come to think of as an oral manner.

(These two attitudes are, respectively, well represented by the dictum, "Whoever forgets a word of his mishnah, scripture accounts it as if he had lost his soul" [Avoth 3:9], and by Ben Sirah's maxim concerning the task of the wise and literate scribe at 39:6). The notion that written and oral discourse are in any sense mutually exclusive, or rigidly to be distinguished (cf. Kelber [1983]), proceeds more from the anthropological abstractions in which some of us are inclined to think, than from an immediate experience of early Judaic sources.

The simple fact of the matter is that orality in early Judaism is, in the nature of the case, evidenced exclusively in written sources, whether of a mishnaic, midrashic, or targumic type. Moreover, interior reference, within these documents, to earlier collections is hardly exceptional. At the level of the initial promulgation of such collections, Neusner (*The Memorized Torah* [1985]) has referred to a process of oral publication: when a teacher's opus achieved a repeatable degree of formality, his halakhah was printed in the memory as carefully as we print our theses on paper. To imagine that we can make any global distinctions between what is "written," and what "oral," is an instance of naïveté bordering on hubris. For precisely that reason, talk of a specifically written "Q," and of multiple recensions of the document misses the point: what we are dealing with is the halakhah of Jesus which, in the prism of transformation and construal, is as multi-faceted (materially speaking) as that of Yoḥanan.

Brian Stock, in his *Implications of Literacy* (1983), has demonstrated conclusively that we have no access to the sense of texts, apart from some familiarity with the community within which those texts function, and with that social function itself. Stock treats of Europe during the twelfth century, when literacy was well established, and written texts were widely produced. But the restriction of literacy to an elite stratum turned the cognitive act of reading into a socially constituitive event: texts became vehicles of socialization, because they were produced, interpreted, and applied according to the elite's principles. Functionally, such principles are promulgated, not by the texts themselves, but within the hermeneutical community, and usually in an oral manner. What Stock has put his finger on, for a particular, textually centered community, is that no society can gain access to its cultural deposit (be it written or oral) apart from an agreed manner of promulgating, interpreting, and applying that deposit, and that tripartite, hermeneutical act is usually conveyed by an oral medium, as is certainly the case in early Judaism and Christianity. No one can know what a document is, much less what to do with it, until he or she has been instructed sufficiently to encounter the literature himself or herself.

The feature that frustrates a purely literary analysis of the canonical literature of both religions, is that their pivotal documents, Mishnah on the one hand, and four Gospels on the other, are -- ab initio -- oral conveyances of meaning, which ultimately achieved written form. (Our conceptual dilemma is only compounded, when we imagine we may limit our attention to "the final form of the text." Such texts, by their very nature, are never final; they are merely received by given communities, and the textual history of variants imitates the dynamic interplay of meanings which produced the documents in the first place.) There is a precise reason for which those documents may be so described: they are not merely cultural deposits, to be interpreted by the tripartite, hermeneutical act described in the last paragraph. During the period which concerns us, Judaism and Christianity accepted the Hebrew Bible (in its own, various forms) as such a deposit, but each developed distinctive hermeneutics for embedding their communities within that deposit, for realizing God's covenant with Abraham. In the case of Mishnah, the hermeneutical act represented is social sanctification by means of the Torah committed to the sages: what is said of the cult and of purity in scripture is, within the mishnaic program, fulfilled in how those who belong to the communities addressed eat, pray, marry, and work (cf. Neusner [1981]). In the case of the Gospels, that act is achieved by appropriating the

halakhah and haggadah of God's son. Neither of these
literatures operates apart from an axiomatic reference
to the Hebrew Bible, and its understanding of
revelation.

Of course, the classic literature of Judaism is
not limited to Mishnah. There is also, in Talmud, the
further evolution of the mishnaic approach, designed
to extend the notion of sanctification beyond the
boundaries initially proposed, so as to address the
issue of how communal integrity is to be preserved, in
the face of Sassanid hegemony to the east, and
Christian imperialism to the west. There is Midrash,
an attempt at relating mishnaic tradition to
scripture; and there is Targum, a related effort, at
speaking scripture with the voice of tradition. What
we have to hand are not genres; the very notion of
"genre" presumes an audience cognizant of literary
forms, with the wherewithal to choose among them in
the marketplace. Rather, variant taxonomies are to
hand, results of the dynamic interaction of cultural
deposit and hermeneutical act, frozen (if only
partially) for a moment in time. That is the literary
lesson of Judaism: a document need not be consigned to
the notion of deposit, but can -- and sometimes must
-- be attended to as the voice of the hermeneutical
process itself.

The effort to discover the "genre" of the
Gospels has been as perennial as it has been
unsuccessful. No document outside the New Testament,
Judaic, hellenistic, discursive, or biographical, has
appeared to establish the existence of a literary form
consistently appropriated or imitated in the Gospels.
The time has come to suggest that there is an
extremely simple reason for this state of affairs: the
Gospels can be assigned to no genre, because they were
not published as literary deposits. They were
promulgated, rather, as hermeneutical acts, which
related the communities for which they were intended
to the covenant with Abraham, which is taken for
granted. The taxonomy of the Gospels is precisely
related to their function, of socializing communities
with the prevalent view of scripture's meaning, and of

socializing scripture within the halakhah and haggadah of Jesus.

An understanding of the taxonomy of the first three Gospels, in particular, provides a perspective from which their synopticity, material and taxic, may be appreciated. Material synopticity, as we have seen in the first three Studies, is a regular feature of documents which share referents to a common tradition of data, thought, and reflection, but which transform and construe that tradition distinctively, in a manner cognate with the taxomony to hand (Mishnah, Tosefta, Yerushalmi, Babli, or Midrash Rabbah). Materially considered, Matthew, Mark, and Luke offer us no more than that degree of congruity with which any student of Rabbinica is familiar, and sometimes they offer us less. But Studies 4 and 5 permitted us to specify, and to find an analogy for, the factor which emerged in the first three Studies as a grave impediment to any direct comparison of the Synoptics with Rabbinica: a taxic synopticity, in which the overarching narrative and the ordering of pericopae within documents relates them, is notably absent in Mishnah, Tosefta, Talmud, and Midrash. The Targumic analogies assessed in the last two studies were, of course, only partial, since an innovative narrative, as the primary, presenting structure, is not at issue in the Targumim. But the consistency of presentation among the Palestinian Targumim is notable, owing to their general program of conveying scripture, and on occasion they evince that very plasticity in ordering which has perennially disturbed students of the Synoptics. Who could guess, for example, that a haggadah of the binding of Isaac would show up at Isaiah 33:7, instead of at Genesis 22 (cf. Chilton [1986]), or that references to the Aqedah would appear sporadically in the Targumim (cf. Davies and Chilton [1978]; Chilton, "Isaac" [1980]; Chilton [1986])? What becomes unmistakably evident, when the Targumim are read, is that taxic synopticity (as distinct from the simple identity which scribal copying might produce, and from the incomparable orders of documents which commonly refer to tradition within different taxonomic programs) is a predictable outcome of reference to congruent traditions by several documents which share a single taxomony.

What, then, is the taxonomy of the Synoptic Gospels? In addition to their common reference to the halakhah and haggadah of Jesus, they share a program of catechetical promulgation. The commonly Synoptic transformation of the kingdom, as we have seen, focuses on Jesus as its herald, advocate, and guarantor, by means of the narrative contextualization of sayings and parables. The christological engine of the Synoptics, that is to say, is systemic, and cannot be reduced to the question of how the titles of Jesus are arranged. Anyone who is convinced by these documents, must either be baptized, or understand what his or her baptism entails, within the pattern of Jesus' teaching, his manner of life, and his vindicated suffering.

Matthew actually keys its close to the continuation of a baptismal movement in Jesus' name (28: 19, 20), but that unique feature of the text comes as no surprise. The Matthean Jesus is, as in none of the other Synoptics, a catechist in the formal sense, who delivers extensive homilies to large groups (5: 1-7: 27), to the select twelve (10), to crowds in the hearing of disciples (13: 1-52), to future leaders of the Church (18), and to disciples with the wit and patience to attend to the end of all things (24-25). Jesus is here an apocalyptic sage, but one whose revelation is grounded carefully in both the scriptures, in the formulaic citations, and in the well marked progress of his own ministry (in teaching, suffering and dying; cf. 4: 17; 16: 21; 26: 16).

The Markan Jesus is more haggadically portrayed, as the relative absence of the halakhic collection known as "Q" would suggest. But the christological engine of Mark is none the weaker for that; on the contrary, the hearer or reader has attention focused all the more on the fact of Jesus' teaching, rather than on what he teaches (cf. France [1980] 102), because the issue of recognition has become paramount. That Jesus is the messiah, God's son, is stated openly from the outset, and is confirmed supernaturally, by voices divine (1: 11; 9: 7) and demonic (1: 24, 34; 3: 11;

5:7), and yet is missed by his contemporaries generally (1:27) and even the disciples (4:41). Peter's confession at Caesarea Philippi is titularly accurate (8:29), and yet it proves to be substantively wrong (vv. 32b-33). At the end of the day, only an anonymous centurion, in the midst of Jesus' suffering, can voice the truth about Jesus in human terms (15:39). The issue of Mark, it seems clear, is catastrophically misconstrued as any "messianic secret," or lack of clarity regarding the identity of Jesus. The ambiguity is only the hearer's or reader's, as he or she comes to decide whether to side with the centurion, or with the high priest, who is told Jesus' identity openly, and does not believe (14:61-62). The Markan Jesus, as in 14:61-62, says what must be said, and yet prefers silence; silence is, in the conditions presumed in this Gospel, a natural feature of that discipleship which understands who Jesus is (16:8).

The Lukan catechesis, of course, extends into the book of Acts, and by doing so betrays the structural nature of its program. To live in diverse communities, from Judea to Rome, with a single scripture, variously translated, and a single, but variegated approach to Jesus, demanded some attempt at synthesis. Luke-Acts obliges with an account which links the activities of Jesus and Paul in a way which advertises their congruity, which establishes the Septuagint as the Bible of the Church, and which openly attempts an accurate ordering of what had been said before (cf. Luke 1:1-4). It is no coincidence that it is precisely this ecclesiastically self-aware corpus which conveys towards its close the content and sense of baptism in the name of Jesus as the recapitulation of what the twelve had enjoyed (Acts 19:1-7). That the Church partakes of the apostolic fullness even as it awaits an indeterminate, but ultimate end, is also attested by Peter (Acts 10:34-43). Luke-Acts establishes baptism as the natural condition of all those who fear God (Acts 10:35).

The distinctiveness of the three Synoptic construals is therefore manifest, as is the underlying integrity of their common transformation. There is no sense in which one can meaningfully be described as a simple repetition of another or others; each conveys what must be conveyed for catechesis in the situation envisaged to succeed. As Dodd (1936) observed, the passage just cited (particularly, Acts 10:36f.) may amount to a précise of the apostolic message. With two qualifications, such a characterization might be welcomed. First, it is apostolic in the functional sense, that it is the version of Jesus' halakhah and haggadah which was standard for catechetical purposes, not in the sense that named apostles can be described as its "authors." That is just the element of Westcott's position which is best dispensed with, despite the tendency of recent discussion. Second, Dodd was inclined to use the term "preaching" rather loosely, as in the present case: Moule (1982) is surely correct in insisting that the Gospels were intended more to instruct than initially to convert those who were totally uninitiated. The apostolic gospel was the catechetical taxonomy, and consequent comparability of taxis, which united the first three Gospels in their mutual reference to the same body of (materially synoptic) tradition.

The necessary distinction between taxic and material synopticity is underlined, when the Synoptics are compared with John and Thomas. Westcott correctly saw that the former Gospel is informed by an alternative dynamic to the Synoptics, but -- without textual warrant -- associated the program with the reminiscence of an individual author. Now that the prolonged development of the Johannine Gospel has been established in recent discussion, we may as firmly reject the myth of "the author" in the case of John as we do in the case of the Synoptics. John's relation with the Synoptics reveals an enduring, material synopticity, but the reference to tradition serves a new, independent taxonomy. The fourth Gospel deliberately sets out a thematic paradigm in its prologue, which focuses on (1) the divinity of "the word," as the foundation of "life" and "light" (1:1-5), (2) the light's attestation by John the Baptist (vv. 6-8), (3) the light's rejection by his own, even as he offered "authority to become God's

children" (vv. 9-13), and (4) the identification of
this light as the word become flesh, the fullest
representation of the divine reality of whose law
Moses is the spokesman (vv. 14-18). The Johannine
blend of halakhah and haggadah required a distinctive
order, and consistent explication, in order to address
precisely those theological issues. Mutatis mutandis,
the Thomaean interlocutions, in their focus on the
correct interpretation of sayings as the mode of entry
into the kingdom, manifest a taxonomy of discourse,
rather than catechesis or theological reflection.

The comparative approach here developed, served
by an understanding of the systemic nature of the
development of tradition into documents in both early
Judaism and Christianity, has brought us to the point
where deviations of one document from another, related
document, are not occasions for perplexity. Rather,
material and taxic synopticity are opportunities, in
which distinctive construals, transformations, and
performances might be observed, in order accurately to
grasp the social function of the meaning conveyed.
Within such an approach, it becomes evident that the
congruent taxonomy of the first three Gospels produced
a common transformation, but variant construals, of
materially cognate tradition. Such material
synopticity is no surprise, within the context of
early Judaism, and may also be instanced in the
relations between the Synoptics on the one hand, and
John and Thomas on the other hand. It is rather the
taxic synopticity of the first three Gospels which
rightly gives the reader pause, and which justifies
their literary characterization as "Synoptics." But
once their commonly and functionally apostolic
taxonomy, as meeting the needs of catechesis, is
appreciated, the source of their agreement (and their
deviation) becomes evident, and insofar as there ever
was a "Synoptic Problem," it may be regarded as
solved.

The fundamental solution, then, resides in
grasping what it is that makes the Synoptic Gospels
synoptic in a distinctive way. Material synopticity in
our texts comes as no surprise, nor are their
manifestations of performances, transformations, and

construals unusual. It is the taxonomies of Matthew,
Mark, and Luke which make them "the Synoptic Gospels,"
because that is the source of their taxic synopticity.
We have referred to the apostolic gospel as the
catechetical taxonomy which makes the Gospels
distinctively synoptic. The periodical presentation of
Jesus as the kingdom's herald, advocate, and guarantor
is symptomatic of that taxonomy.

Those three phases of the taxonomy,
corresponding to major phases in the Gospels, are
themselves susceptible of analysis. This is not the
place (or the time) to engage in anything like a
consideration of the taxonomic constituents of the
Synoptics, but the main lines of such an analysis
might be suggested. The portrayal of Jesus as the
kingdom's herald would necessarily include his own
preaching of the kingdom, and probably his call of
disciples. It also referred to John the Baptist, and
could include (as in Matthew and Luke) the birth of
Jesus, and even of John (so Luke). Once Jesus was
identified as the herald of the kingdom, the
transmission of haggadah and halakhah in his name
would represent his advocacy of the kingdom. ("Q" is
the name for the relative non-use of halakhic material
in Mark.) But the framing of this complex material by
the scenes of Jesus' baptism and transfiguration
suggests it was actively proleptic of the passion, the
final constituent of the taxonomy. Indeed, that would
explain why, in recent research, the question of where
the narratives of the passion began has caused
controversy. It could end, of course, with (so Matthew
and Luke) or without (so Mark) stories concerning the
appearance of Jesus as risen. Once it is understood
that the commonly catechetical taxonomy operated
within an environment in which material synopticity
was natural, constituting a transformation of that
tradition, we have as much a "solution" to "the
Synoptic Problem" as we will ever have, and at the
same time, we allow that the particular construals of
Matthew, Mark, and Luke -- in terms of scribal
catechesis, silent discipleship, and ecclesial
eschatology -- each attests the literarily historical
Jesus.

APPENDICES

Appendix I

Bekharoth 5a

שאל קונטרוקוס השר את רבן יוחנן בן זכאי בפרטן של לוים
אתה מוצא עשרים ושנים אלף ושלש מאות בכללן אתה מוצא
עשרים ושנים אלף ושלש מאות להיכן הלכו א"ל אותן שלש
מאות בכורות היו ואין בכור מפקיע בכור .

Sanhedrin 1:4 (Yerushalmi)

אנטונינות הגמון שאל את רבן יוחנן בן זכאי בכלל חסירין
ופוט יתירין אמר ליה אותן שלש מאות יתירין בכורי
כהונה היו אין קודש מוציא קודש .

Numbers Rabbah 4:9

וזו שאלה שאל הונגטיס הגמון לרבן יוחנן בן זכאי אמר
לו משה רבכם או גנב היה או לא היה יודע לחשב אמר לו
למה אמר לו הונגטיס מפני שהיו עשרים ושנים אלף בכורות
ועוד מאתים ושבעים ושלשה וצוה המקום שיפדו הלוים
בבכורו הן עשרים ושנים אלף של לוים כנגד עשרים ושנים
אלף בכורות ועוד נמצאו בלוים יתרים על עשרים ושנים
אלף שלש מאות כמו שהוא מחשב במנין ראשון בפרטן מפני
מה אותן שלש מאות הלוים לא פדו אותן מאתים ושבעים
ושלשה בכורות העוד פין על עשרים ושנים אלף בכורות
שאנו מוצאים שאותן מאתים ושבעים ושלשה נותנין חמשה
חמשה סלעים ועוד מפני מה כשכלל מנין הלוים בסוף מפני
מה פחת מהן שלש מאות מן מנין ראשון הוי לא גנב אותן
מן החשבון אלא כדי שיהנו אותן מאתים ושבעים ושלשה
בכורות חמשה חמשה סלעים לאהרן אחיו או שמא לא היה ידע
לחשב אמר לו ר' יוחנן בן זכאי לא גנב היה ויודע היה
לחשב ודבר אחד לחש לי לומר לך אמר לו אמר אמר לו ר'
יוחנן בן זכאי ידע את לקרות אבל אין את יודע לדרש אמר
אותן עשרים ושנים אלף של לוים פודין לעשרים ושנים אלף
של בכורות נשתירו בלוים עוד שלש מאות בכורות עוד
מאתים ושבעים ושלשה והיו אותן שלש מאות שבלוים בכורות
ואין בכור פודה בכור לפיכך משה מנה אותן גנבן מפני
שהיו בכורות מיד נסתלק ממנו

Statistics:

Bekharoth/Sanhedrin--
1=68%
d (Bekharoth)=46%
d (Sanhedrin)=68%
s=71%
average=62%.

Bekharoth/Numbers Rabbah--
1=17%
d (Bekharoth)=84%
d (Numbers Rabbah)=14%
s=68%
average=46%.

Sanhedrin/Numbers Rabbah--
1=12%
d (Sanhedrin)=56%
d (Numbers Rabbah)=7%
s=57%
average=33%.

Matthew 19:3-12

καὶ προσῆλθον αὐτῷ Φαρισαῖοι πειράζοντες αὐτὸν καὶ
λέγοντες εἰ ἔξεστιν ἀνθρώπῳ ἀπολῦσαι τὴν γυναῖκα
αὐτοῦ κατὰ πᾶσαν αἰτίαν; ὁ δὲ ἀποκριθεὶς εἶπεν οὐκ
ἀνέγνωτε ὅτι ὁ κτίσας ἀπ' ἀρχῆς ἄρσεν καὶ θῆλυ
ἐποίησεν αὐτούς; καὶ εἶπεν ἕνεκα τοῦτο καταλείψει
ἄνθρωπος τὸν πατέρα καὶ τὴν μητέρα καὶ κολληθήσεται
τῇ γυναικὶ αὐτοῦ καὶ ἔσονται οἱ δύο εἰς σάρκα μία.
ὥστε οὐκέτι εἰσὶν δύο ἀλλὰ σὰρξ μία ὃ οὖν ὁ θεός
συνέζευξεν ἄνθρωπος μὴ χωριζέτω. λέγουσιν αὐτῷ τί
οὖν Μωϋσῆς ἐνετείλατο δοῦναι βιβλίον ἀποστασίου καὶ
ἀπολῦσαι αὐτήν; λέγει αὐτοῖς ὅτι Μωϋσῆς πρὸς τὴν
σκληροκαρδίαν ὑμῶν ἐπέτρεψεν ὑμῖν ἀπολῦσαι τὰς
γυναῖκας ὑμῶν ἀπ' ἀρχῆς δὲ οὐ γέγονεν οὕτως. λέγω
δὲ ὑμῖν ὅτι ὃς ἂν ἀπολύσῃ τὴν γυναῖκα αὐτοῦ μὴ ἐπὶ
πορνείᾳ καὶ γαμήσῃ ἄλλην μοιχᾶται.
    λέγουσιν αὐτῷ οἱ μαθαταὶ αὐτοῦ εἰ οὕτως ἐστὶν ἡ
αἰτία τοῦ ἀνθρώπου μετὰ τῆς γυναικός οὐ συμφέρει
γαμῆσαι. ὁ δὲ εἶπεν αὐτοῖς οὐ πάντες χωροῦσιν τὸν

λόγον τοῦτον ἀλλ' οἷς δέδοται. εἰσὶν γὰρ εὐνοῦχοι
οἵτινες ἐκ κοιλίας μητρὸς ἐγεννήθησαν οὕτως καὶ
εἰσὶν εὐνοῦχοι οἵτινες εὐνουχίσθησαν ὑπὸ τῶν
ἀνθρώπων καὶ εἰσὶν εὐνοῦχοι οἵτινες εὐνούχισαν
ἑαυτοὺς διὰ τὴν βασιλείαν τῶν οὐρανῶν. ὁ δυνάμενος
χωρεῖν χωρείτω.

Mark 10:2-12

καὶ ἐπηρώτων αὐτὸν εἰ ἔξεστιν ἀνδρὶ γυναῖκα
ἀπολῦσαι πειράζοντες αὐτόν. ὁ δὲ ἀποκριθεὶς εἶπεν
αὐτοῖς τί ὑμῖν ἐνετείλατο Μωϋσῆς; οἱ δὲ εἶπαν
ἐπέτρεψαν Μωϋσῆς βιβλίον ἀοστασίου γράψαι καὶ
ἀπολῦσαι. ὁ δὲ Ιησοῦς εἶπεν αὐτοῖς πρὸς τὴν
σκληροκαρδίαν ὑμῶν ἔγραψεν ὑμῖν τὴν ἐντολὴν ταύτην
ἀπὸ δὲ ἀρχῆς κτίσεως ἄρσεν καὶ θῆλυ ἐποίησεν
αὐτούς. ἕνεκεν τούτου καταλείψει ἄνθρωπος τὸν
πατέρα αὐτοῦ καὶ τὴν μητέρα καὶ προσκολληθήσεται
πρὸς τὴν γυναῖκα αὐτοῦ καὶ ἔσονται οἱ δύο εἰς σάρκα
μίαν ὥστε οὐκέτι εἰσὶν δύο ἀλλὰ μία σάρξ ὅ οὖν ὁ
θεὸς συνέζευξεν ἄνθρωπος μὴ χωριζέτο.
    καὶ εἰς τὴν οἰκίαν πάλιν οἱ μαθηταὶ περὶ τούτου
ἐπηρώτων αὐτόν καὶ λέγει αὐτοῖς ὃς ἂν ἀπολύσῃ τὴν
γυναῖκα αὐτοῦ καὶ γαμήσῃ ἄλλην μοιχᾶται ἐπ' αὐτήν.
καὶ ἐὰν αὐτὴ ἀπολύσασα τὸν ἄνδρα αὐτῆς γαμήσῃ ἄλλον
μοιχᾶται.

Luke 16:18

πᾶς ὁ ἀπολύων τὴν γυναῖκα αὐτοῦ καὶ γαμῶν ἑτέραν
μοιχεύει καὶ ὁ ἀπολελυμένον ἀπο ἀνδρὸς γαμῶν
μοιχεύει.

Statistics:

  Matthew/Mark--
  l=68%
  d (Matthew)=51%
  d (Mark)=75%

s=74%
average=67%.

Matthew/Luke--
l=9%
d (Matthew)=7%
d (Luke)=71%
s=23%
average=28%.

Mark/Luke--
l=13%
d (Mark)=12%
d (Luke)=88%
s=27%
average=33%.

Appendix II

Tosephta Sotah 13:3

עד שיחיו המתים משמת חגי זכריה ומלאכי נביאים
האחרונים פסקה רוח הקודש מישראל ואף על פי כן היו
משמיעין להן בבת קל מעשה שנכנסו חכמי לבית גוריו
ביריחו ושמעו בת קל אום יש כאן אדם שראוי לרוח הקודש
אלא שאין דורו זכאי לכך ונתנו עיניהם בהילל הזקן
וכשמר אמרו עלו הי עניו הי חסיד תלמיד של עזרא.

Sanhedrin 11a:

ת"ר משמתו נביאים האחרונים חגי זכריה ומלאכי נסתלקה
רוח הקודש מישראל ואף על פי כן היו משתמשים בבת קול
פעם אחת היו מסובים בעלייה בית גוריה ביריחו ונתנה
עליהם בת קול מן השמים יש כאן אחד שראוי שתשרה עליו
שכינה כמשה רבינו אלא שאין דורו זכאי לכך נתנו חכמים
את עיניהם בהלל הזקן וכשמת אמרו עליו הי חסיד הי עניו
תלמיד של עזרא.

Sotah 48b:

דת"ר משמתו חגי זכריה ומלאכי נסתלקה רוח הקודש
מירשראל ואע"ף כן היו משתמשים בבת קול שפעם אחת

מסובים בעליית בית גוריא ביריחו נתנה עליהן בת קול מן
השמים ואמרה יש בכם אדם אחד שרחי שהשרה שכינה עליו
אלא שאין דורו ראוי לכך נתנו עיניהם בהלל הזקן וכממת
הספידוהו הי חסיד הי עניו תלמיד של עזרא.

Sotah 9:13 (Yerushalmi):

משמתו נביאים האחרונים הגי זכריה ומלאכי פסקה מהן רוח
הקודש אף על פי כן משתמשין היו בבת קול מעשה ששמע
שמעון הצדיק בת קול יוצא מבית קודש הקדשים ואמר נהרג
גייסגוליקס ובטלו גזירותיו מעשה שיצאו נערים להלחם
באנטוכיא ושמע יוחנן כהן גדל בת קול יוצא מבית קודש
הקדשים ואמרת נצחו טלייא דאגחו קרבא באנטוכיא וכהם
אותה העת ונתנו בו זמן וכיוונו שבאותה שעה היתה מעשה
שנכנסו זקנים אצל בית גדיא ביריחו ויצתה בת קול ואמרה
להן יש ביניכם אדם אחד ראוי לרוח הקודש אלא שאין הדור
כדיי ונתנו עיניהן בהלל הזקן וכשמת היו אומרים עליו
הוי עניו חסיד תלמידו של עזרא.

Appendix III

Shebi'ith 9:1 (Yerushalmi):

כ"ש בן יוחי עביד טמיר במערתא תלת עשר שנין במערת
חרובין דתרומה עד שהעלה גופו חלודה לסיף תלת עשר שנין
אמר לינה נפיק חמי מה קלא עלמא נפיק ויתיב ליה על
פומא דמערתא חמא חד צייד צייד ציפרין פרס מצודוי שמע
ברת קלא אמרה דימוס ואישתיזב ציפור אמר ציפור מבל עדי
שמי לא יבדא כ"ש בר נשא.

Appendix IV

Further discussion is available in *Gospel
Perspectives* I (ed. R. T. France and D. Wenham;
Sheffield: JSOT, 1980) 21-45, an article reprinted
in *Targumic Approaches to the Gospels*, 113-135.
Unfortunately, Moses Ginsburger does not offer this
passage in *Das Fragmententhargum* (Berlin: Calvary,
1899), but cf. Bishop Walton's Polyglot (London:

1655-1657), Le Déaut's *La nuit pascale:* Analecta Biblica 22 (Rome: Pontifical Biblical Institute, 1963, 1975) and J. W. Etheridge's translation (New York: Ktav, 1968) for the text here postulated. Cf. the edition by M. L.Klein, *The Fragment Targums of the Pentateuch according to their Extant Sources:* Analecta Biblica 76 (Rome: Biblical Institute, 1980). Klein's edition of Ms Vatican Ebr. 440 largely agrees with earlier work in respect of this passage, but there are certain important differences. Klein has the messiah come "from Rome," rather than "from above." His reading is the more plausible if, as in his ms, "flock" replaces "cloud," although his reading cannot be considered certain (as discussed in the review mentioned in the main text.) Lastly, after "both," Klein reads, "and I and they lead together." Effectively, a text closer to Neophyti is what Klein presents, unlike the readings of other witnesses. The situation would seem to justify the propriety of a synoptic approach to the study of Targumim.

In the case of Neophyhti I, we offer the following version on the basis of Díez Macho's editio princeps (Madrid: Consejo Superior de Investigaciones científicas, 1970):

It is a night to be observed and set aside for redemption to the name of the LORD in the time he brought forth those of the sons of Israel, freed from the land of Egypt. Indeed, these four nights are written in the book of memorials. The first night, when the LORD was revealed upon the world to create it, and the world was without form and void and darkness was spread on the face of the deep, and the LORD's memra was light and enlightened; he called it the first night.

The second night, when the LORD was revealed upon Abraham, a hundred years old, and Sarah his wife, ninety years old, to establish what scripture says, will Abraham, a hundred years old, beget, and will Sarah his wife, ninety years old, bear?

And Isaac was thirty-seven years old when he was offered on the altar. The heavens descended and came down and Isaac saw their perfections, and his eyes were darkened from their perfections, and he called it the second night.

The third night, when the Lord was revealed upon the Egyptians at the dividing of the night; his hand killed the firstborn of the Egyptians and his right hand shielded the firstborn of Israel, to establish what scripture says, Israel is my firstborn son, and he called it the third night.

The fourth night, when the end of the age is accomplished to be redeemed, the iron yokes broken and the generations of wickedness destroyed. Moses comes up from the desert. One leads in the head of the flock, and the other leads at the head of a flock, and his memra leads them both, and I and they lead together.

This is the night of passover to the name of the LORD, to be observed and set aside for redemption by all Israel in their generations.

The translations of the Fragments Targum and Neophyti here presented are designed to give the reader opportunity to compare more deviations than are discussed in the main text. "The other" in Neophyti refers to a missing antecedent, such as the messiah (cf. Díez Macho, pp. 78, 79).

Appendix V

The texts within Study 5 were first discussed in *JBL* 101 (1982) 553-562 (also available in *Targumic Approaches to the Gospels*, 137-149). The editions consulted include those of Díez Macho, Ginsburger, Klein, and Rieder.

BIBLIOGRAPHY

K.   Aland,   *Synopsis   Quattuor   Evangeliorum...*
(Stuttgart: Würtembergische Bibelanstalt, 1967)

P. S. Alexander, Review of *A Galilean Rabbi and His
Bible*, *Journal of Jewish Studies* 36 (1985) 238-242

D. Barthelémy, *Les devanciers d'Aquila. Première
publication intégrale du texte des fragments du
Dodécaphrophéton trouvés dans le desert de Juda...*
(Leiden: Brill, 1963)

R. Bauckham, "The Liber Antiquitatum Biblicarum of
Pseudo-Philo and the Gospels as 'Midrash'," *Gospel
Perpsectives III. Studies in Midrash and
Historiography* (ed. R.T. France and D. Wenham;
Sheffield: JSOT, 1983)

G.R. Beasley-Murray, *Jesus and the Kingdom of God*
(Grand Rapids: Eerdmans, 1986)

K. Berger, *Die Gesetzauslegung Jesu. Ihr historischer
Hintergrund im Judentum und im Alten Testament:* WMANT
40 (Neukirchen-Vluyn: Neukirchener Verlag, 1972)

K. Beyer, *Semitische Syntax im Neuen Testament:*
Studien zur Umwelt des Neuen Testaments 1 (Göttingen:
Vandenhoeck und Ruprecht, 1968)

P. Billerbeck, *Kommentar zum Neuen Testament aus
Talmud und Midrasch* (München: Beck, 1922-1961)

T. Boman, *Die Jesus-Überlieferung im Lichte der
neueren Volkskunde* (Göttingen: Vandenhoeck und
Ruprecht, 1967)

———————, *Gemeindebildungen im Neuen Testament*
(Göttingen: Vandenhoeck und Ruprecht, 1967)

M. Borg, "A Temperate Case for a Non-Eschatological
Jesus," *Forum* 2 (1986) 81-102

G. Bornkamm, G. Barth, H.J. Held (tr. P. Scott), *Tradition and Interpretation in Matthew:* New Testament Library (Philadelphia: Westminster, 1963

J. W. Bowker, "The Son of Man," *Journal of Theological Studies* 28 (1977) 19-48

J.P. Bowman, "The Form of 'Q' known to Matthew," *New Testament Studies* 8 (1961-61) 27-42

-----------, "Mark as Witness to an Edited Form of Q," *Journal of Biblical Literature* 80 (1961) 29-44

M. Brocke, W. Petuchowski, and W. Strolz, *Das Vaterunser. Gemeinsames im Beten von Juden und Christen:* Veröffentlichungen der Stiftung Oratio Dominica (Freiburg: Herder, 1974), cf. *The Lord's Prayer and Jewish Liturgy* (New York: Seabury, 1978)

R. E. Brown, *The Gospel according to John:* The Anchor Bible (Garden City: Doubleday, 1966, 1970).

R. Bultmann (tr. J. Marsh), *The History of the Synoptic Tradition* (New York: Harper and Row, 1968)

-----------, *Jesus Christ and Mythology* (New York: Scribner's, 1958)

----------- (tr. L. P. Smith and E. Huntress), *Jesus and the Word* (New York: Scribner's, 1934)

T. A. Burkill, *Mysterious Revelation. An Examination of the Philosophy of St Mark's Gospel* (Ithaca: Cornell University Press, 1963)

W. Bussmann, *Synoptische Studien* (Halle: Waisenhauses, 1925-1931)

B. C. Butler, *The Originality of St Matthew. A Critique of the Two-Document Hypothesis* (Cambridge: Cambridge University Press, 1951)

G. B. Caird, *Saint Luke:* The Pelican New Testament Commentaries (Harmondsworth: Penguin, 1972)

O. Camponovo, *Königtun: Königsherrschaft und Reich Gottes in den frühjüdischen Schriften:* (Göttingen: Vandenhoeck und Ruprecht, 1984)

J. Carmignac, *Le Mirage de l'Eschatologie. Royauté, Règne et Royaume de Dieu...sans Eschatologie* (Paris: Letouzey et Ané, 1979)

B. H. Childs, *The New Testament as Canon: An Introduction* (Philadelphia: Fortress, 1985)

B. D. Chilton, "'Amen': an Approach through Syriac Gospels," *Zeitschrift für die neutestmantliche Wissenschaft* 69 (1978) 203-211, and *Targumic Approaches,* 15-23

----------, *A Galilean Rabbi and His Bible. Jesus' Use of the Interpreted Scripture of His Time:* Good News Studies 8 (Wilmington: Glazier, 1984) and (with a different subtitle) SPCK (London: 1984)

----------, *The Glory of Israel. The Theology and Provenience of the Isaiah Targum:* Journal for the Study of the Old Testament Supplement 23 (Sheffield: *Journal for the Study of the Old Testament,* 1982)

----------, *God in Strength. Jesus' Announcent of the Kingdom:* Studien zum Neuen Testament und seiner Umwelt 1 (Freistadt: Plöchl, 1979), reprinted in The Biblical Seminar of JSOT (Sheffield: 1987)

----------, "The Gospel according to Thomas as a Source of Jesus' Teaching," *Gospel Perspectives 5. The Jesus Tradition Outside the Gospels* (ed. D. Wenham; Sheffield: *Journal for the Study of the Old Testament,* 1984)

----------, "Isaac and the Second Night: a Consideration," *Biblica* 61 (1980) 78-88, and *Targumic Approaches,* 25-37

-----------, *The Isaiah Targum. Introduction, Translation, Apparatus, and Notes:* The Aramaic Bible (Wilmington: Glazier, 1987)

----------- (ed.), *The Kingdom of God in the Teaching of Jesus:* Issues in Religion and Theology 5 (Philadelphia: Fortress, 1984)

-----------, "Recent Discussion of the Aqedah," *Targumic Approaches,* 39-49

-----------, "Regnum Dei Deus Est, *Scottish Journal of Theology* 31 (1978) 261-270, and *Targumic Approaches,* 99-107

Review of *Geniza Manuscripts of Palestinian Targum to the Pentateuch, Journal of Biblical Literature* 107 (1988) 772-775

-----------, *Targumic Approaches to the Gospels. Essays in the Mutual Definition of Judaism and Christianity:* Studies in Judaism (Lanham, New York, London: University Press of America, 1986)

-----------, "The Transfiguration: Dominical Assurance and Apostolic Vision," *New Testament Studies* 27 (1980) 115-124

-----------, "Varieties and Tendencies of Midrash: Rabbinic Interpretations of Isaiah 24:23," *Gospel Perspectives III* (cf. Bauckham), 9-32

B. D. Chilton and J. I. H. McDonald, *Jesus and the Ethics of the Kingdom:* Biblical Foundations in Theology (London: SPCK, 1987 and [out of series] Grand Rapids: Eerdmans, 1988)

D. J. A. Clines, *The Theme of the Pentateuch:* Journal for the Study of the Old Testament Supplement 10 (Sheffield: JSOT, 1978)

H. Conzelmann (tr. G. Buswell), *The Theology of St Luke* (London: Faber and Faber, 1961)

C. E. B. Cranfield, *The Gospel according to St Mark* (Cambridge: Cambridge University Press, 1959)

P. R. Davies and B. D. Chilton, "The Aqedah: a Revised Tradition History," *Catholic Biblical Quarterly* 40 (1978) 514-546

M. Dibelius (tr. B. L. Woolf), *From Tradition to Gospel* (New York: Scribner's, 1935)

A. Díez Macho, *Neophyti I. Genesis* (Madrid: Consejo Superior de Investigaciones científicas, 1968); *Exodus*, in the same series (1970)

C. H. Dodd, *The Apostolic Preaching and Its Developments. Three Lectures with an Appendix on Eschatology and History* (London: Hodder and Stoughton, 1936)

F. G. Downing, "Redaction Criticism: Josephus' *Antiquities* and the Synoptic Gospels (II)," *Journal for the Study of the New Testament* 9 (1980) 29-48

J. Drury, Review of *The Evangelists' Calendar, Journal for the Study of the New Testament* 7 (1980) 71-73

--------, *The Parables in the Gospels. History and Allegory* (New York: Crossroad, 1985)

--------, *Tradition and Design in Luke's Gospel. A Study in Early Christian Historiography* (London: Darton, Longman and Todd, 1976)

R. A. Edwards, *A Theology of Q. Eschatology, Prophecy, and Wisdom* (Philadelphia: Fortress, 1976)

P. Ellingworth, "Text and Context in Mark 10:2, 10," *Journal for the Study of the New Testament* 5 (1979) 63-66

H. Falk, *Jesus the Pharisee. A New Look at the Jewishness of Jesus* (New York: Paulist, 1985)

W. R. Farmer, *The Synoptic Problem. A Critical Analysis* (Dillsboro: Western North Carolina Press, 1976)

A. M. Farrer, "On Dispensing with Q," *Studies in the Gospels. Essays in Memory of R. H. Lightfoot* (ed. D. E. Nineham; Oxford: Blackwell, 1955) 55-86

------------, *St Matthew and St Mark* (Westminster: Dacre, 1954)

J. A. Fitzmyer, "Another View of the 'Son of Man' Debate," *Journal for the Study of the New Testament* 4 (1979) 58-68

--------------, *The Gospel According to Luke I-IX. Introduction, Translation, and Notes:* The Anchor Bible (Garden City: Doubleday, 1981)

D. Flusser, *Die rabbinischen Gleichnisse und der Gleichniserzähler Jesus: Judaica et Christiana* 4 (Bern: Peter Lang, 1981)

R.T. France, "Mark and the Teaching of Jesus," *Gospel Perspectives I. Studies of History and Tradition in the Four Gospels* (ed. France and D. Wenham; Sheffield: JSOT, 1980) 101-136

E. Fuchs (tr. A. Scobie), *Studies of the Historical Jesus:* Studies in Biblical Theology 42 (Naperville: Allenson, 1964)

B. Gerharsson, Memory and Manuscript. Oral Tradition and Written Transmission in Rabbinic Judaism and Early Christianity: Acta Seminarii Neotestamentici Upsaliensis (Lund: Gleerup, 1961)

M. Ginsburger, *Pseudo-Jonathan* (Berlin: Calvary, 1903)

T. F. Glasson, "Schweitzer's Influence: Blessing or Bane?" *The Kingdom of God* (ed. Chilton, 1984) 107-20

M. Goulder, *The Evangelists' Calendar. A Lectionary Explanation of the Development of Scripture* (London: SPCK, 1978)

E. Grässer, "On Understanding the Kingdom of God," *The Kingdom of God* (ed. Chilton, 1984) 52-71

M. Green, *The Empty Cross of Jesus:* The Jesus Library (London: Hodder and Stoughton, 1984)

H. Greeven, *Synopsis of the First Three Gospels* (Tübingen: Mohr, 1981)

P. Grelot, "Les Targums du Pentateuque: Etude comparative d'après Genèse IV, 3-16," *Semitica* 9 (1959) 59-88

J. J. Griesbach, "Commentatio qua Marci Evangelium totum e Matthaei et Lucae commentariis decerptum esse monstratur," *J. J. Griesbach: Synoptic and Text-critical Studies 1776-1976:* Society of New Testament Studies Monograph Series 34 (Cambridge: Cambridge University Press, 1978)

--------------, *Synopsis Evangeliorum Matthaei, Marci et Lucae...* (Halle, 1776)

J. R. Harris, "Traces of Targumism in the New Testament," *Expository Times* 32 (1920-21) 373-76

J. C. Hawkins, *Horae Synopticae. Contributions to the Study of the Synoptic Problem* (Oxford: Clarendon, 1909, reprinted in 1968)

M. Higger, *Treatise Semaḥoth* (New York: Bloch, 1931)

E. Hirsch, *Frühgeschichte des Evangeliums...* (Tübingen: Mohr, 1941)

BIBLIOGRAPHY

P. Hoffmann, *Studien zur Theologie der Logienquelle: Neutestamentliche Abhandlungen* 8 (Münster: Aschendorff, 1972)

H. J. Holtzmann, *Die synoptischen Evangelien. Ihr Ursprung und geschichtlicher Charakter* (Leipzig: Engelmann, 1863)

J. Jeremias (tr. S. H. Hooke), *The Parables of Jesus* (London: SCM, 1972)

L. E. Keck, *A Future for the Historical Jesus. The Place of Jesus in Preaching and Theology* (Nashville: Abingdon, 1971)

----------, "The Introduction to Mark's Gospel," *New Testament Studies* 12 (1965-66) 352-70

W. H. Kelber, *The Kingdom in Mark. A New Place and a New Time* (Philadelphia: Fortress, 1974)

------------, *The Oral and Written Gospel. The Hermeneutics of Speaking and Writing in the Synoptic Tradition, Mark, Paul, and Q* (Philadelphia: Fortress, 1983)

J. D. Kingsbury, *Matthew: Structure, Christology, Kingdom* (London: SPCK, 1976)

M. L. Klein, *The Fragment Targums of the Pentateuch according to their Extant Sources:* Analecta Biblica 76 (Rome: Biblical Institute, 1980)

----------, *Geniza Manuscripts of Palestinian Targum to the Pentateuch* (Cincinatti: Hebrew Union College Press, 1986)

K. Koch, "Messias und Sündenvergebung in Jesaja 53--Targum. Ein Beitrag zu der Praxis der aramäischen Bibelübersetzung," *Journal of Semitic Studies* 3 (1972) 117-148

T. S. Kuhn, *The Structure of Scientific Revolutions* (Chicago: University of Chhicago, 1962)

G. J. Kuiper, "Targum Pseudo-Jonathan: A Case Study of Genesis 4:7-10, 16," *Augustinianum* 10 (1970) 533-70

W. G. Kümmel, "Jesusforschung seit 1965: Nachträge 1975-1980," *Theologische Rundschau* 47 (1982) 136-65

---------- (tr. S. M. Gilmour and H. C. Kee), *The New Testament. The History of the Investigation of Its Problems* (London: SCM, 1973)

---------- (tr. D. M. Barton), *Promise and Fulfillment. The Eschatological Message of Jesus:* Studies in Biblical Theology 23 (Naperville: Allenson, 1957)

G. E. Ladd, *The Presence of the Future. The Eschatology of Biblical Realism* (Grand Rapids: Eerdmans, 1974)

W. L. Lane, *The Gospel according to Mark:* The New London Commentary (London: Marshall, Morgan, and Scott, 1974)

M. Lattke, "On the Jewish Background of the Synoptic Concept, 'The Kingdom of God'," *The Kingdom of God* (ed. Chilton, 1984) 72-91

R. Le Déaut, *La nuit pascale:* Analecta Biblica 22 (Rome: Pontifical Biblical Institute, 1963)

B. Lindars, *Jesus, Son of Man. A fresh examination of the Son of Man sayings in the Gospels in the Light of Recent Research* (Grand Rapids: Eerdmans, 1983)

----------, *New Testament Apologetic. The Doctrinal Significance of Old Testament Quotations* (Philadelphia: Westminster, 1961)

M. McNamara, *Targum and Testament. Aramaic Paraphrases of the Hebrew Bible. A Light on the New Testament* (Shannon: Irish University Press, 1972)

A. H. McNeile, *The Gospel according to St. Matthew* (London: Macmillan, 1915)

A. Marmorstein. "Einige vorläufige Bemerkungen zu den neuentdeckten Fragmenten des jerusalemischen (palästinischen) Targums," *Zeitschrift für die alttestamentliche Wissenschaft* 49 (1931) 225-37

J. Marsh, *The Book of Numbers:* The Interpreter's Bible (New York: Abingdon, 1953)

I. H. Marshall, *The Gospel of Luke. A Commentary on the Greek Text* (Paternoster: Exeter, 1978)

--------------, *Luke. Historian and Theologian* (Exeter: Paternoster, 1970)

W. Marxsen (tr. R. A. Harrisville and others) *Mark the Evangelist. Studies in the Redaction History of the Gospel* (New York: Abingdon, 1969)

A. J. Mattill, *Luke and the Last Things. A Perspective for the Understanding of Lukan Thought* (Dillsboro: Western North Carolina Press, 1979)

W. A. Meeks, *The Prophet-King. Moses Traditions and the Johannine Christology:* Supplements to Novum Testamentum 14 (Leiden: Brill, 1967)

H. Merklein, *Jesu Botschaft von der Gottesherrschaft:* Stuttgarter Bibelstudien 3 (Stuttgart: Katholisches Bibelwerk, 1983)

L. Miller and M. Simon, *Bekharoth:* The Babylonian Talmud (London: Soncino, 1949)

M. A. Mirkin, *Midrash Rabbah* 9 (Tel-Aviv: Yavneh, 1964)

R. Morgenthaler, *Statistische Synopse* (Zürich: Gotthelf, 1971)

C. F. D. Moule, *The Birth of the New Testament* (San Francisco: Harper and Row, 1982 cf. also Longdon: Black, 1966 and 1982)

E. Nestle and others, *Novum Testamentum Graece* (Stuttgart: Deutsche Bibelstiftung, 1979)

J. N. Neusner, *The Bavli and Its Sources. The Question of Tradition in the Case of Tractate Sukkah:* Brown Judaic Studies 85 (Atlanta: Scholars Press, 1987)

------------, *Judaism. The Evidence of Mishnah:* Chicago Studies in the History of Judaism (Chicago: University of Chicago Press, 1981)

------------, *The Memorized Torah. The Mnemonic System of Mishnah:* Brown Judaic Studies 96 (Chico: Scholars Press, 1985)

------------, *Midrash as Literature. The Primacy of Documentary Discourse:*Studies in Judaism (Lanham, New York, London: University Press of America, 1987)

------------, *The Peripatetic Saying. The Problem of the Thrice-Told Tale in Talmudic Literature:* Brown Judaic Studies 89 (Chico: Scholars, 1985)

------------, "The Synoptic Problem in Rabbinic Literature: The Cases of the Mishnah, Tosepta, Sipra, and *Leviticus Rabba,*" *Journal of Biblical Literature* 105 (1986) 499-507

------------, *The Tosefta translated from the Hebrew. Third Division: Nashim* (New York: Ktav, 1979)

H. Odeberg, *The Aramaic Portions of Bereshit Rabba with Grammar of Galilean Aramaic:* Lunds Universitets Arsskrift 36.3 (Lund: Gleerup, 1939)

M. P. Parasis (publisher), *Bekharoth min Talmud Babli* (Jerusalem: 5723)

------------, *Sanhedrin min Talmud Babli* (Jerusalem: 5757)

------------, *Sotah min Talmud Babli* (Jerusalem: 5724)

------------, *Talmud Yerushalmi* (Jerusalem: 5726, 5727)

N. Perrin, *Jesus and the Language of the Kingdom. Symbol and Metaphor in New Testament Interpretation* (London: SCM, 1976)

---------, *Rediscovering the Teaching of Jesus* (New York: Harper and Row, 1967)

---------, *What is Redaction Criticism?* (Philadelphia: Fortress, 1969)

H. Räisänen, *Das "Messiasgeheimnis" im Markusevangelium. Ein redaktionskritischer Versuch* (Helsinki: Schriften der Finnischen Exegetischen Gesellschaft, 1976)

B. Reicke, *The Roots of the Synoptic Gospels* (Philadelphia: Fortress, 1982)

D. Rieder, *Pseudo-Jonathan* (Jerusalem: Salmon, 1974)

R. Riesner, "Der Ursprung der Jesus-Uberlieferung," *Theologische Zeitschrift* 38.6 (1982) 493-513

J. M. Rist, *On the Independence of Matthew and Mark:* SNTSMS 32 (Cambridge: Cambridge University Press, 1978)

J. M. Robinson, *A New Quest for the Historical Jesus and Other Essays* (Philadelphia: Fortress, 1982)

J. A. T. Robinson, *The Priority of John* (London: SCM, 1985)

W. Sanday, "On the Nature of Miracle," *Divine Overruling* (Edinburgh: Clark, 1920) 53-81

----------(ed.), *Studies in the Synoptic Problem. By Members of the University of Oxford* (Oxford: Clarendon, 1911)

P. Schäfer, "Bibelübersetzungen II. Targumim," *Theologische Realenzyklopädie* VI.1,2 (ed. G. Krause and G. Müller; Berlin: de Gruyter, 1980) 216-28

------------, *Die Vorstellung vom heiligen Geist in der rabbinischen Literatur:* Studien zum Alten und Neuen Testament 28 (Munich: Kösel, 1972)

K. L. Schmidt, *Der Rahman der Geschichte Jesu. Literarkritische Untersuchungen zur ältesten Jesus-Uberlieferung* (Berlin: Trowitzsch, 1919)

S. Schulz, *Q. Der Spruchquelle der Evangelisten* (Zürich: Theologischer Verlag, 1972)

H. Schürmann, *Das Lukasevangelium. Erstes Teil. Kommentar zu Kap. 1,1-9,50:* Herders theologischer Kommentar zum Neuen Testament (Freiburg: Herder, 1969)

B. B. Scott, *Jesus. Symbol-Maker for the Kingdom* (Philadelphia: Fortress, 1981)

A. Schweitzer (tr. W. Montgomery), *The Quest of the Historical Jesus. A Critical Study of its Progress from Reimarus to Wrede* (London: Black, 1954)

P.L. Shuler, *A Genre for the Gospels. The Biographical Character of Matthew* (Philadelphia: Fortress, 1982)

M. Smith, "A Comparison of Early Christian and Early Rabbinic Tradition," *Journal of Biblical Literature* 82 (1963) 169-176

--------, *Tannaitic Parallels to the Gospels:* Journal of Biblical Literature Monograph Series 6 (Philadelphia: Journal of Biblical Literature, 1951)

H. F. D. Sparks, *A Synopsis of the Gospels. The Synoptic Gospels with the Johannine Parallels* (Philadelphia: Fortress, 1964)

D. W. Staerk, *Altjüdische liturgische Gebete. Ausgewählt und mit Einleitung:* Kleine Texte (Bonn: Marcus und Weber, 1910)

V. H. Stanton, *The Jewish and Christian Messiah. A Study in the Earliest History of Christianity* (Edinburgh: Clark, 1886)

R. H. Stein, "The 'Criteria' for Authenticity," *Gospel Perspectives* (see under France), 225-263

-----------, "The Proper Methodology for Ascertaining a Markan Redaction History," *Novum Testamentum* 13 (1971) 181-198

G. Stemberger, *Die römische Herrschaft im Urteil der Juden:* Erträge der Forschung 195 (Darmstadt: Wissenschaftliche Buchgesellschaft, 1983)

B. Stock, *The Implications of Literacy. Written Language and Models of Interpretation in the Eleventh and Twelfth Centuries* (Princeton: Princeton University Press, 1983)

D. F. Strauss, *Das Leben Jesu, kritisch bearbeitet* (Tübingen: Osiander, 1835, 1836)

J. F. Stenning, *Targum to Isaiah* (Oxford: Clarendon, 1949)

B. H. Streeter, *The Four Gospels. A Study of Origins* (London: Macmillan, 1924)

--------------, "On the Original Origin of Q," "St. Mark's Knowledge and Use of Q," "The Original Extent of Q," "The Literary Evolution of the Gospels," in Sanday (1911), 141-164, 165-183, 185-208, 209-227

-------------- (with A. J. Appasamy), *The Sadhu: A Study in Mysticism and Practical Religion* (London: Macmillan, 1921)

G. M. Styler, "Excursus IV. The Priority of Mark" in Moule, 285-316 and 223-232 (respectively, in the two editions)

V. Taylor, *The Gospel according to St Mark* (London: Macmillan, 1952)

A. C. Thiselton, *The Two Horizons. New Testament and Philosophical Description with Special Reference to Heidegger, Bultmann, Gadamer, and Wittgenstein* (Grand Rapids: Eerdmanns, 1980)

W. Trilling, *Das Wahre Israel. Studien zur Theologie des Matthäus-Evangeliums:* Studien zum Alten und Neuen Testament 10 (Munich: Kösel, 1964)

C. M. Tuckett, *The Revival of the Griesbach Hypothesis. Analysis and Appraisal:* SNTSMS 44 (Cambridge: Cambridge University Press, 1983)

G. Vermes, *Jesus and the World of Judaism* (London: SCM, 1983)

---------, *Jesus the Jew. A Historian's Reading of the Gospels* (London: Collins, 1973)

---------, "'The Son of Man' Debate," *Journal for the Study of the New Testament* 1 (1978) 19-32

---------, "The Targumic Versions of Genesis IV 3-16," *Annual of the Leeds University Oriental Society* 3 (1960-61) 81-114

210   BIBLIOGRAPHY

B. T. Viviano, *Study as Worship. Aboth and the New Testament:* Studies in Judaism in Late Antiquity (Leiden: Brill, 1978)

W. O. Walker, *The Relationship among the Gospels. An Interdisciplinary Dialogue:* Trinity University Monograph Series in Religion 5 (San Antonio: Trinity University Press, 1978)

J. Wenham, *Easter Enigma. Do the Resurrection stories contradict one another?* (Exeter: Paternoster, 1984)

B. F. Westcott, *The Gospel according to St John* (London: Murray, 1890)

--------------, *Introduction to the Study of the Gospels with Historical and Explanatory Notes* (New York: Macmillan, 1896)

-------------- and F. J. A. Hort, *The New Testament in the Original Greek* (London: Macmillan, 1901)

J. W. Wevers and U. Quast, *Numeri:* Septuaginta (Göttingen: Vandenhoeck und Ruprecht, 1982)

W. Wrede, *Das Messiasgeheimnis in den Evangelien. Zugleich ein Beitrag zum Verständnis des Markusevangelium* (Göttingen: Vandenhoeck und Ruprecht, 1901), translated under the title *The Messianic Secret* by J. C. G. Greig (Greenwood: Attic, 1971)

M. S. Zuckermandel, *Tosephta based on the Erfurt and Vienna Codices* (Jerusalem: Wahrman, 1970)

Scriptures

Genesis
1:1-5 -- 108
1:3 -- 114
1:27 -- 61, 67
2:24 -- 61, 67
4:8 -- 123, 124, 125-131
15:17 -- 108, 113, 114
17:17 -- 108
22:1-18 -- 108
23:1 -- 108
27:1 -- 108
28:15 -- 85

Exodus
4:22 -- 109, 110
12:29 -- 109
12:42 -- 107-115
24:1, 2 -- 82
24:1-8 -- 81
24:9 -- 81
24:9-11 -- 82
24:10 -- 81, 86
24:10, 11 -- 117
24:11 -- 81, 86
24:12-14 -- 82
24:15 -- 81
24:16 -- 81
24:17, 18 -- 81
24:18 -- 82
33:18-23 -- 118
33:20 -- 86
33:23 -- 86
34:29, 30 -- 86

Numbers
3:14-37 -- 49
3:22 -- 49
3:28 -- 49
3:34 -- 49, 52
3:34-51 -- 56
3:39 -- 49, 51, 53, 54, 59

Antiquities
4.8.48 @ 326 -- 84
9.2.2 @ 28 -- 84
18.5.2 @ 118 -- 142

Mishnah (M.), Tosefta (T.), Yerushalmi (Y.), Bavli,
and Midrash Rabbah:
M. Avoth 1:1 -- 79, 174
Babba Metzia 59a, b -- 78
Berakoth 4b, 5a -- 53
5b -- 49-51, 53, 55, 58, 59, 74
Ecclesiastes Rabbah 10:8 -- 92, 93
Genesis Rabbah 79:6 -- 92, 93
M. Gittin 9:10 -- 61
M. Kethuboth 5:5 -- 68
           7:2-5, 9-10 -- 68
Kiddushin 49a -- 117, 118
Megillah 32a -- 105
M. Nedarim 11:12 -- 68
Numbers Rabbah 3:14 -- 55, 56
4:9 -- 55, 56, 58, 59, 74
Sanhedrin 11a -- 79
         152b -- 141, 143, 144, 151
         153a -- 141, 143, 147, 148, 151
Y. Sanhedrin 1:4 -- 54, 58, 59
Shabbath 31a -- 74
Y. Shebi'ith 9:1 -- 91, 93
Sotah 33 -- 80
      33a -- 80
      48b -- 79
T. Sotah 13:3 -- 77, 78
         13:5 -- 80
         13:7 -- 80
Y. Sotah 9:13 -- 5, 79

Matthew
1:1-17 -- 19
3:1-6 -- 19
3:7-10 -- 18
3:11-12 -- 19
3:13-15 -- 20
3:13-17 -- 19
3:17 -- 17

Scholars

Lachmann -- 27, 28, 29
Lane -- 67
Le Déaut -- 110
Lindars -- 95
Marmorstein -- 135
Marsh -- 52
Mattill -- 158
McDonald -- 147
McNamara -- 106, 117, 121
Meeks -- 89
Merklein -- 140
Moule -- 180
Nathan -- 144
Neusner -- 49, 50, 53, 54, 59, 77, 79, 80, 82, 151, 152, 168, 174, 175
Odeberg -- 94-96
Papias -- 15, 17
Petuchowski -- 146
Qontroquos -- 49-51, 53, 54, 57
Reicke -- 44, 170
Resh Laqish -- 53
Riches -- 172
Rist -- 106, 170
Robinson -- 106
Sanday -- 27, 29, 30, 32, 34, 35, 43, 44, 45, 168, 169, 171
Schäfer -- 77, 124
Schmidt -- 43
Schulz -- 15
Schweitzer -- 99
Simeon ben Yoḥai -- 91-94, 96, 102, 103, 139, 163
Smith -- 45, 106, 119
Staerk -- 146
Stanton -- 171
Stein -- 161
Stemberger -- 53, 54
Stenning -- 105, 106
Stock -- 174
Strack--Billerbeck -- 45
Strauss -- 27
Streeter -- 13, 14, 16, 22, 23, 28, 29, 31, 34, 35, 36, 37, 38, 39, 40, 42, 43, 169, 171
Styler -- 12

Brown Judaic Studies

140001	*Approaches to Ancient Judaism I*	William S. Green
140002	*The Traditions of Eleazar Ben Azariah*	Tzvee Zahavy
140003	*Persons and Institutions in Early Rabbinic Judaism*	William S. Green
140004	*Claude Goldsmid Montefiore on the Ancient Rabbis*	Joshua B. Stein
140005	*The Ecumenical Perspective and the Modernization of Jewish Religion*	S. Daniel Breslauer
140006	*The Sabbath-Law of Rabbi Meir*	Robert Goldenberg
140007	*Rabbi Tarfon*	Joel Gereboff
140008	*Rabban Gamaliel II*	Shamai Kanter
140009	*Approaches to Ancient Judaism II*	William S. Green
140010	*Method and Meaning in Ancient Judaism*	Jacob Neusner
140011	*Approaches to Ancient Judaism III*	William S. Green
140012	*Turning Point: Zionism and Reform Judaism*	Howard R. Greenstein
140013	*Buber on God and the Perfect Man*	Pamela Vermes
140014	*Scholastic Rabbinism*	Anthony J. Saldarini
140015	*Method and Meaning in Ancient Judaism II*	Jacob Neusner
140016	*Method and Meaning in Ancient Judaism III*	Jacob Neusner
140017	*Post Mishnaic Judaism in Transition*	Baruch M. Bokser
140018	*A History of the Mishnaic Law of Agriculture: Tractate Maaser Sheni*	Peter J. Haas
140019	*Mishnah's Theology of Tithing*	Martin S. Jaffee
140020	*The Priestly Gift in Mishnah: A Study of Tractate Terumot*	Alan. J. Peck
140021	*History of Judaism: The Next Ten Years*	Baruch M. Bokser
140022	*Ancient Synagogues*	Joseph Gutmann
140023	*Warrant for Genocide*	Norman Cohn
140024	*The Creation of the World According to Gersonides*	Jacob J. Staub
140025	*Two Treatises of Philo of Alexandria: A Commentary on De Gigantibus and Quod Deus Sit Immutabilis*	David Winston/John Dillon
140026	*A History of the Mishnaic Law of Agriculture: Kilayim*	Irving Mandelbaum
140027	*Approaches to Ancient Judaism IV*	William S. Green
140028	*Judaism in the American Humanities*	Jacob Neusner
140029	*Handbook of Synagogue Architecture*	Marilyn Chiat
140030	*The Book of Mirrors*	Daniel C. Matt
140031	*Ideas in Fiction: The Works of Hayim Hazaz*	Warren Bargad
140032	*Approaches to Ancient Judaism V*	William S. Green
140033	*Sectarian Law in the Dead Sea Scrolls: Courts, Testimony and the Penal Code*	Lawrence H. Schiffman
140034	*A History of the United Jewish Appeal: 1939-1982*	Marc L. Raphael
140035	*The Academic Study of Judaism*	Jacob Neusner
140036	*Woman Leaders in the Ancient Synagogue*	Bernadette Brooten
140037	*Formative Judaism: Religious, Historical, and Literary Studies*	Jacob Neusner
140038	*Ben Sira's View of Women: A Literary Analysis*	Warren C. Trenchard
140039	*Barukh Kurzweil and Modern Hebrew Literature*	James S. Diamond